PIKES PEAK
COUNTRY

FALCON™

PIKES PEAK
COUNTRY

About the Author

Jim Scott is an outdoor writer specializing in wildlife, fishing, and western history topics. He has worked for the U.S. Forest Service and the Colorado Division of Wildlife, and his writing has appeared in such publications as *Colorado Outdoors, Nature,* and *Colorado Monthly* magazine. An admitted fishing fanatic, Jim spends much of his free time along the streams and lakes of the Rocky Mountain West. He currently lives with his wife Georgia in Boulder, Colorado.

Acknowledgments

A host of people go into the creation of any book. I would first like to thank the staff members of the following institutions: the Carnegie Branch of the Boulder Public Library, the University of Colorado's Norlin Library (Western Historical Collections and Rare Books sections), the Western History Department of the Denver Public Library, the Colorado Historical Society, the Penrose Municipal Library in Colorado Springs, the Canon City Municipal Library, and the Canon City Municipal Museum.

Some of the individuals who greatly aided me in the completion of the text include Duncan Rollo and the entire staff at Florissant Fossil Beds National Monument, Jim Hekkers and Bob Hernbrode from the Colorado Division of Wildlife, Curt Buchholtz and the members of the Rocky Mountain Nature Association, geologist Sue Raabe (who took the time to show me the country), and Wendy Shattil,

Bob Rozinski, Stewart Green, Ken Smith, Dave Elson, Chuck Baynton, Joe O'Laughlin, Jerry Craig, Russ Bromby, Steve Bissell, Kevin Fitzgerald, Eddie Kochman, and Tom Swanson. Thanks especially to Georgia, my wife, and Jesse for their unflagging encouragement and support.

The Rocky Mountain Nature Association

The Rocky Mountain Nature Association played a vital role in the publication of this book. The RMNA is a nonprofit organization that supports educational and research programs within Rocky Mountain National Park, Florissant Fossil Beds National Monument, and neighboring national forests. The association sells books, maps, and other interpretive items to help visitors understand park features and values. In addition to funding naturalist programs and research, the RMNA also sponsors seminars each summer on the human and natural history of the parks and publishes books and maps to aid educational programs and management. All RMNA activities are supported solely by sales income, memberships, and contributions. For more information contact the Rocky Mountain Nature Association, Rocky Mountain National Park, Estes Park, Colorado, 80517.

Dedication

This book is dedicated to Colorado's staggering and irreplaceable natural resources, lest we ever forget.

Scott, James A., 1946-
    Pikes Peak country / by Jim Scott.—Helena, Montana. : Falcon Press, c1987.
    97, [7] p. : col. ill., ports. ; 22 x 28 cm.—(Colorado geographic series ; no. 3)

    Bibliography: p. [99].
    ISBN 1-56044-249-2

    1. Pikes Peak (Colo.)—Description and travel. 2. Pikes Peak (Colo.)—Pictorial works. I. Title. II. Series.

F782.P63S37 1987   978.8'56—dc19   86-82747
                                          AACR 2 MARC

Front cover photo

Pikes Peaks' 14,110-foot summit dominates the skyline west of Colorado Springs, photo by Michael S. Sample.

Back cover photos

Top right: wasp fossil at Florissant, photo by Leo L. Larson; balsamroot, photo by Michael S. Sample; solitary horseback rider, photo by Stewart M. Green.

Published by Falcon Press Publishing Co., Inc., in cooperation with the Rocky Mountain Nature Association.

Design, typesetting, and other prepress work by Falcon Press, Helena, Montana.

Printed in Korea.

Contents

Aspen leaves in Horsethief Park, near Pikes Peak, pour from the sky like golden rain during October windstorms. STEWART M. GREEN

The view west from the north slopes of Pikes Peak encompasses range after range of Fourteeners. CHARLES KNOECKEL

Pikes Peak or Bust!

Standing as it does on the edge of the Front Range of the Southern Rocky Mountains, aloof and alone, Pikes Peak is the singular beacon to one of the most stunning regions in Colorado. A landmark, lodestone, and sentinel of granite, the massive mountain casts an imposing shadow.

At 14,110 feet, Pikes Peak is by no means the highest of the state's 54 Fourteeners, ranking a distant thirty-first behind 14,433-foot Mount Elbert. But because of its geographic position, rising like a behemoth apparition over the eastern plains, the storied peak has had a significant influence on the region historically, culturally, and economically.

Its visibility to travelers has made it so. Wayfarers from the south can first distinguish it with the naked eye from Raton Pass in New Mexico some 150 miles away. From Greeley, 100 miles to the north, it can be seen jutting out from the Front Range.

It was the view from the east, however, that captured America's imagination. In 1806 a 26-year-old newly commissioned lieutenant in the U.S. Army named Zebulon Pike was assigned the task of leading an exploratory survey party deep into the recently acquired Louisiana Purchase to explore its southern boundaries and to search for the headwaters of the Red River.

On November 6, from a point near the present-day town of Holly (a few miles from the Kansas border), Pike first caught sight of the mountain. Later that evening he recorded the events of the day in his journal.

"Marched early," he wrote. "Passed two deep creeks and many high points of rocks; also large herds of buffalo. At two o'clock in the afternoon I thought I could distinguish a mountain to our right, which appeared like a small blue cloud; viewed it with a spyglass, and was still more confirmed in my conjecture. . . . "

Grasses like these will provide forage for deer and elk during the long, harsh winter months.
STEPHEN TRIMBLE

Although the peak now bears his name, he was by no means the mountain's discoverer. The Ute Indians, who had for centuries known the mountain as "the Long One," passed under its shadow regularly during their summer pilgrimages from "the Boiling Springs" (Manitou Springs) to South Park, their favored big game hunting grounds.

The Spanish, too, knew of the mountain long before Pike. Coronado may well have seen it on his 1541 expedition through the Southwest in search of the elusive Seven Cities of Gold, and other Spanish adventurers undoubtedly encountered the peak, most notably Juan De Anza, who even traversed its flanks in 1779. Some of what the eighteenth century Spanish in the region knew of the mountain apparently came from French trappers, who had begun trickling into present-day Colorado by that time.

Pike set the stage, however, for the eventual settling of the western United States. The host of explorers who followed on his heels, including Stephen Long (1820), Colonel Henry Dodge (1835), and John C. Fremont (1843), made significant historical inroads of their own into the area. The intoxicating influence of Pikes Peak was not felt,

however, until gold fever swept the country in the late 1850s.

When William Green Russell discovered gold on Dry Creek in 1858 near Denver, the word was out. A major strike on Clear Creek west of Denver near Georgetown the following year hastened a rush from the East, causing an estimated 100,000 fortune seekers to set out for Colorado territory during a three-month period. Although only about half of them reached their destination, this may have been the most significant event in the history of the state.

The much-publicized lodes actually lay over 100 miles to the north of Pikes Peak, but people from all over the country focused on the huge mountain. Those opting to roll their dice and livestock westward even advertised their destination on the sides of their prairie schooners with the slogan ''Pike's Peak or Bust.''

This obsession was documented by the *St. Louis News* in a story published on March 13, 1859. ''It is astounding how fast we learn geography. A short time since, we hardly knew, and didn't care whether the earthly elevation called Pike's Peak was in Kansas or Kamchatka. Indeed, ninety-nine out of every one-hundred persons in the country did not know there was such a topographical feature as Pike's Peak.

''Now they hear of nothing, dream of nothing, but Pike's Peak. It is the magnet to the mountains, toward which everybody and everything is tending. It seems that every man, woman and child, who is going anywhere at all, is moving Pike's Peakward.''

For the fortune seekers, the mountain was definitely the draw, albeit a misguided one. Today, however, it is the region itself that is magnetic, attracting residents and visitors alike with an uncanny allure.

Its resources are diverse, providing wilderness and history, fossils and wildflowers, rivers and spires, gorges and wildlife. Pikes Peak Country is an adventure in geology, paleontology, ecology, and culture.

To obtain a sense of where you are, there is no better place than from the top of Pikes Peak. Today, hundreds of thousands of people intent on the region literally take it from the top each year, ascending Pikes Peak on foot, by car, or by cog railway. This conglomeration of tourists on the mountain's alpine summit would undoubtedly have surprised Pike, who fell some 15 miles short in his attempt to reach it because of snow and concluded that under such conditions ''no human being could have ascended its pinical [sic].''

Most who reach the top today are surprised by the weather there. Although it appears serene and appealing on a typical summer's day, the summit has a cold, harsh climate ill-suited to most living things. It can snow during any month (and often does), and the winds and electrical storms that batter the top are a frightening lesson in meteorology. But the view, combined with the altitude, can leave one literally gasping.

To the northwest of Zebulon Pike's ''Great Peak'' lie the Florissant Valley, Lake George, and the salt flats of South Park. JACK OLSON

That is apparently what happened in 1893 when Katherine Lee Bates, a visiting professor from Wellesley College, took time out from a summer of teaching at Colorado College to visit the top by carriage. Deeply moved, she descended with the inspiration for "America the Beautiful." The "amber waves of grain" were the Great Plains to the east, and the "purple mountain's majesty" was, of course, the great peak itself.

Today, a view towards the grain fields begins with a look at Colorado Springs, which spills from the foothills of the Front Range onto the eastern plains. A failing gold camp in the late 1860s, the metropolitan area today boasts more than 400,000 people, second only to Denver in size.

Colorado Springs now dominates Pikes Peak Country culturally and economically. Colorado College, which was founded in 1874, and the University of Colorado at Colorado Springs, which held its first classes in 1967, are today renowned as two of the finest institutions of higher learning in the state. Museums, art and sports centers, high-tech industry, and tourist attractions permeate the metropolis.

The military influence is also strong. The U.S. Air Force Academy and Fort Carson flank Colorado Springs on the north and south, respectively. Deep under Cheyenne Mountain, the North American Air Defense Command (NORAD) monitors the world's airspace. At Peterson Air Force Base, the U.S. Space Command Center now hums night and day.

In the northwest corner of the city, tucked in a valley below the natural barrier of the Rampart Range, lies the Garden of the Gods, Colorado Springs' most striking natural feature next to Pikes Peak. A wind- and water-sculpted gallery of towering sandstone monoliths, mushrooms, and balanced rocks, it holds a fascination for residents, tourists, and geologists alike.

From a point adjacent to the Garden, Ute Pass, which follows a natural fault line and was the favored trail of the Indians to South Park, climbs steeply to Woodland Park, a natural gateway to the mountains.

Directly west of the peak, 10 miles as the crow flies, is 12,000-acre Mueller State Park. Managed for both wildlife and recreation, the park is a haven

for black bears, mountain lions, elk, deer, golden eagles, wild turkeys, bobcats, and Rocky Mountain bighorn sheep. The geologic outcropping of Dome Rock, which towers over the park, is similar to the famous Half Dome in California's Yosemite National Park.

Several miles north of Mueller State Park is the Florissant Fossil Beds National Monument, one of the least known and most astonishing of Colorado's natural resources. Here visitors can literally peer into a window on the past some 35 million years ago when volcanic ash and mud flows settled over the area and froze in time much of the life in the semitropical lake bed.

Today, enormous petrified tree stumps as well as one of the richest repositories of plant and insect fossils in the world testify to life in the Oligocene Epoch. To paleontologists and amazed visitors, the Florissant fossil beds are a treasure from a time long past.

Far to the northwest of Pikes Peak, past Divide, Florissant, Lake George, and Hartsel, the South Platte River tumbles from its headwaters atop the Continental Divide. Although only a trickle at birth, the South Platte and its tributaries will be corralled by seven reservoirs on their journey to Denver and beyond.

The Pikes Peak Cog Railway, which reached the top of Pikes Peak in 1891, is one way tourists reach the second-most-visited summit in the world. Only the top of Mt. Fuji in Japan has hosted more people. JACK OLSON

From South Park, the river plunges from Elevenmile Reservoir into the photogenic Elevenmile Canyon. Pike knew well of both the park and canyon; after making a brief excursion up Elevenmile Canyon in search of the headwaters of the Red River, he set off across South Park, relentless if misguided. To the northeast, the South Platte twists through a landscape of ponderosa pine and granite, pools at Cheesman Lake, and finally slices through Cheesman Canyon. The steeply walled gorge, littered with enormous boulders and deep, clear pools, is an angler's dream. The natural productivity of the waters in the canyon has helped to create the finest trout fishery near a major metropolitan area anywhere in the lower 48 states.

Due west of Cheesman Canyon, hidden between the Tarryall and Kenosha mountains, lies the Lost Creek Wilderness Area. A granitic kaleidoscope of twisting spires, castles, and mosques, the area is named for the waterways that meander in and out of the formations, periodically disappearing underground only to pop up unexpectedly farther downstream. Because of its relative inaccessibility to all but the most dedicated hikers, the Lost Creek Wilderness Area has remained one of the wildest areas in the state.

Some 10 miles due southwest of the peak, the Cripple Creek-Victor mining district sits astride a huge volcanic depression. Although the gold rush in the Pikes Peak region during the late 1850s was less profitable than the claims above Denver, an unbelievable strike at Cripple Creek late in 1890 by a cowboy named Bob Womack turned Pikes Peak Country upside down.

In short order, the tiny district with its 500 residents swelled to more than 55,000, producing more than $340 million worth of gold over the next several decades. A thriving tourist community today that now features legal, limited-stakes gambling, the Cripple Creek-Victor area is renowned for its autumn extravaganza of changing aspens and its boomtown heritage.

South of Cripple Creek, the little-traveled dirt Shelf Road weaves through spectacular Helena Canyon, no doubt one of the most scenic rides in Colorado. Breaking out of the hills at Garden Park, it becomes Fourmile Creek Road and passes an abandoned quarry, a common sight in the region.

But this quarry, carved from Morrison Formation sandstone, is different. It held one of the richest dinosaur fossil deposits ever discovered in the United States, yielding the gigantic remains of such specimens as brontosaurus, tyrannosaurus, and stegosaurus. First excavated in 1877, the Garden Park Quarry stands as one of the most significant paleontological sites ever discovered.

Canon City, eight miles south of Garden Park, is the second-largest town in the Pikes Peak region. Quiet and pretty, it has more the aura of a midwestern community than an Eastern Slope city. Although a center of cherry and apple growing and the site of Colorado's state penitentiary, Canon City is best known as the gateway to the awesome Royal Gorge.

A result of the unrelenting Arkansas River shearing through more than 1,000 feet of solid granite, the Royal Gorge initially blocked Pike's route west in 1806. Today it is perhaps the most singularly spectacular sight in the Pikes Peak region. Visitors can view the canyon from several perspectives. They can drive over it across the world's highest suspension bridge, walk down the foot trails that lead to the bottom, or ride on board the world's steepest incline railway.

From nearby Florence, which mirrors Canon City in its charm, Phantom Canyon runs north into the mountains of the Cripple Creek district. Known as "the Gold Belt Line" during the Cripple Creek boom, the route (now Highway 67) once boasted three trains daily each way. Today, in addition to its natural beauty, Phantom Canyon is a classic study in ecology, containing three different life zones and a host of wildlife habitats. The incredible spectacle of autumn foliage in the canyon makes the road one of the most traveled in the region.

Returning again to the top of Pikes Peak, the headwaters of Beaver Creek trickle off the south end of the mountain. Far down on the flanks of 10,096-foot Black Mountain, the Beaver Creek Wilderness Study Area stretches across 26,150 acres of some of the most rugged country of Colorado's Front Range.

Gold Camp Road, an original railroad route, loops around the peak's eastern and southern shoulders to the Cripple Creek district. Known as the "Short Line" during the gold boom, Gold

Camp Road today is the most direct automobile route from Colorado Springs to the famous gold camps. The stupendous drive past the upheaved granite spires and domes of Cathedral Park was perhaps best described by Theodore Roosevelt, who traveled it in the early 1900s. Its spectacular scenery, Teddy concluded, "is such as to bankrupt the English language."

The splendor of Pikes Peak Country, from the alpine wildflowers atop the great peak to the mysterious Precambrian granite, ever exposed by the Arkansas River in the depths of the Royal Gorge, is a collection of geologic miracles, ghosts of the past, wildland, and hardy people. But what is Pikes Peak Country, and where does it end?

Pikes Peak Country is not a series of longitudes and latitudes on a map, nor is it bordered by mountain ranges, rivers, or fault lines. It is in the mind.

Indeed, who will tell the wheat farmer in Crowley County, wiping the sweat from his brow as he gazes up at the peak nearly 60 miles across the Great Plains, that he is not a resident of Pikes Peak Country? Or the businesswoman in Castle Rock, who commutes into Denver each morning so that she might drive home each evening in full view of the mountain, that she, too, is not in Pikes Peak Country?

And what of the visitors to the region? Back home now, are these travelers out of range of Pikes Peak's magnetic hold? Likely not. Like a lucky amulet, memories of the region are invariably carried over the miles and through the years, immune to the weathering of distance and time. Pikes Peak Country, above all else, is a place in the heart.

A broken-down shantytown little more than a century ago, the humming metropolis of Colorado Springs has become a cultural, tourist, high-tech, and military center.
ROBERT MACKINLAY

Hikers on the eastern slope of Pikes Peak ascend via the Barr Trail, hammered out with pickaxes and blasting powder in the early part of the century. STEWART M. GREEN

A geological tour

Looking at the Front Range rising west over Colorado Springs, it is hard to believe that these majestic mountains are not at all eternal. In fact, they are relatively new, at least Colorado's third set of mountains.

Colorado is tough on its mountains. They are either being uplifted by tremendous underground forces, remodeled by volcanoes, scrubbed by glaciers, or erased by erosion. The earliest mountains from billions of years ago and the more recent Ancestral Rockies from merely hundreds of millions went through uplifts, stood for ages, and were ultimately rubbed away by wind and water as cleanly as chalk from a slate.

Happily for geologists, paleontologists, rock climbers, miners, and sightseers, some outstanding examples of the geologic legacy of these events— Pikes Peak, the Garden of the Gods, Cripple Creek, the Royal Gorge, and Florissant—have given Pikes Peak Country a rich endowment.

Pikes Peak

Pikes Peak began forming over a billion years ago. Deep in the earth, 20 miles or so, it started as an immense mass of molten rock or magma that later solidified into a batholith. By definition, a batholith must measure at least 40 square miles. At 2,000 square miles—roughly the size of Delaware—the Pikes Peak batholith easily met the criterion.

It first emerged at the earth's surface 650 to 700 million years ago, where it was later covered by the great seas that engulfed Colorado. The batholith re-emerged 350 million years ago as a part of the Ancestral Rockies, then was eroded to sea level and flooded over once again. It reappeared 60 million years ago during the Laramide Orogeny, a period of massive uplift of ancient rocks from Mexico to Alaska that created the modern Rockies, and rose to an elevation of about 3,000 feet.

About 7 to 10 million years ago, in conjunction

Saxifrage, left, an alpine wildflower, grows sheltered in the granite of Pikes Peak. STEPHEN TRIMBLE

Interlocking crystals of glass-like quartz, below, combined with pink feldspar and black mica, give the coarse Pikes Peak granite its beautiful reddish hue. MICHAEL S. SAMPLE

Pikes Peak at sunrise in the Garden of the Gods. TOM ALGIRE

with a later dramatic uplifting of all the Colorado Rockies, the ever-massive Pikes Peak batholith began rising skyward to reach its present elevation of 14,110 feet. Pikes Peak is still rising, in fact, by precious centimeters annually.

The mountain did not achieve its present shape immediately. Beginning about 2 million years ago, with the advent of the Pleistocene Ice Age, glaciers gouged, scraped, and beveled its flanks to give Pikes Peak its familiar appearance.

The basic principle of glaciation is simple enough. When more snow falls in the winter than can be melted in the summer, glaciers are born. From the mountain's upper elevations of 12,500 to 14,000 feet, they crept down the slopes, coming to rest at about 9,000 feet.

The key to the glaciers' actions was motion. As they built up in the deeper ravines, the ice crystals froze to the rock walls. When they started to move, only inches a day in the summer and even less in the winter, the glaciers pulled down the rock faces of the canyon walls, leaving distinctive hollows called cirques. The Crater, perhaps the best known cirque on Pikes Peak, lies between Cameron Cone and the summit and is clearly visible from Colorado Springs. The 1,700-foot-deep Bottomless Pit, directly north of the peak's apex, is another.

As these moving tongues of ice traveled, they deepened and widened the canyons in great U-shaped patterns, scouring the bedrock underneath with sandpaper-like efficiency. The rubble of

broken rocks that the glaciers carried along left a clear trail. These tracks, called lateral moraines, are visible on several walls of the glaciated valleys of Pikes Peak, including the Crater. Melting and evaporation at approximately 9,000 feet halted the glaciers' progress, leaving telltale piles of rocky and sandy rubble called moraines. One of the best examples is at Lake Moraine, on the mountain's southeast side. The lake, or tarn, was formed about 7,000 years ago when a glacier melted and left behind a dam of rubble marking the end of Colorado's last ice age.

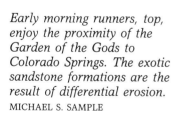

Early morning runners, top, enjoy the proximity of the Garden of the Gods to Colorado Springs. The exotic sandstone formations are the result of differential erosion.
MICHAEL S. SAMPLE

Pikes Peak, at right, viewed here from the Garden of the Gods, was formed from a batholith which emerged hundreds of millions of years ago. STEWART M. GREEN

Garden of the Gods

Balanced Rock, perhaps the best-known monument in the Garden of the Gods, looks as if it might topple from its perch at any moment. So convincing is the illusion, in fact, that it seems every third or fourth tourist who wanders by (and thousands do each day during the summer months) persuades a companion to photograph him in the exaggerated pose of holding back the massive block of sandstone from tumbling onto the road.

The Garden of the Gods, an 824-acre park owned by the city of Colorado Springs, is said to resemble a slumping shelf of books, with volumes scattered awry in all directions. The wildly tilted towers and incongruous rock formations, which delight rock climbers and tourists alike, have been given whimsical names like Baby Elephant, Kissing Camels, Stagecoach and Horses, Weeping Indian, and Rocking Chair.

Ferdinand Vandeveer Hayden, who visited the area in 1869 for the U.S. Geological Survey of the Territories, was impressed. "Around Colorado Springs," he wrote later in his report to Congress, "there is a tract of ten miles square, containing more materials of geologic interest than any other area of equal extension in the West."

The story of the Garden of the Gods begins about 300 million years ago, when Frontrangia (a part of the Ancestral Rockies) was being dismantled through the action of constant weathering and a halt in its uplifting. The ancient rivers of the region carried rocks and debris from the shrinking mountain range east and spread it out over the Colorado Springs area in great alluvial fans hundreds of feet thick.

This material, the Fountain Formation, was covered by shallow seas for most of the next 150 million years, then dried by the sun and wind as the seas receded. The result was a series of cement-like, fossil-bearing sandstone and mud-stone conglomerates, reddened by ferric iron and strongly crisscrossed with ripple marks. These layers, the Lyons, Morrison, and Dakota formations, are evidence of the seas, beaches, and swamps that once covered Colorado.

As the last seas withdrew, a tremendous upheaval took place in central Colorado about 60 million years ago during the Laramide Orogeny. The Garden is located directly on top of the volatile and ancient Rampart Range Fault. When uplift began, the fault was activated, and the horizontal rock layers that once lay on the sea floor began doming, then shattered and tilted skyward, bowing to the underlying pressure of the fault. This stretching, arching, and crumbling—which seems nearly audible when described in words—actually took place quietly, over the course of millions of years. During that time, new alluvial fans built out over the incipient Garden of the Gods to bury the fractured rocks under the Dawson formation. After that, no new rocks were deposited and a long period of erosion began.

Much later, perhaps 7 million years ago, renewed movements along the base of the Front Range elevated and upended the rocks and exposed them directly to erosion, thus beginning the construction of the characteristic spires, balanced rocks, towers, and mushroom-shaped rocks seen today.

The key to the exotic and bizarre formations in the Garden is the differential erosion that has taken place in the sedimentary rocks. The more resistant monuments are tall, squat, pointed, rounded, or generally baffling; the less resistant ones were long ago reduced to valleys and flats. What remains today is the stuff of storybooks.

Cripple Creek

Just as Pikes Peak was physically shaped by geologic forces, its history was shaped by mineralization. For eons, the precious metals lay untouched, locked in the rocks below the surface. In the course of the last century their presence or absence, as determined by frantic mining activity, dictated the patterns of settlement and the economy of Pikes Peak Country.

At an elevation of 9,000 feet and nine miles west of Pikes Peak, the Cripple Creek mining district is laid out within a volcanic crater-like depression known as a diatreme. In its glory, the area was the richest goldfield in Colorado. More than half of the gold and silver mined from the state came out of the Cripple Creek-Victor area, the bulk of it between 1891 and 1916. All told, some 27 tons of fine gold (a $420 million bonanza back then) were excavated from the holes at Cripple Creek.

Nearly as surprising, the strikes came in a tiny

Birth of a garden

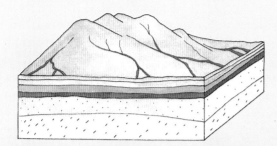

About 350 million years ago, the Ancestral Rockies towered over much of Colorado. The easternmost chain of these peaks, known as Frontrangia, was located some 30 to 50 miles west of the present-day Front Range. As they do today, the waterways in the region drained to the east.

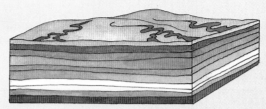

A pause 300 million years ago in the uplifting process, coupled with relentless erosion, began wearing down the Ancestral Rockies. Rubble from this erosion was distributed over the Colorado Springs area in enormous alluvial fans.

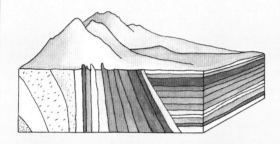

Some 60 million years ago, the modern Rocky Mountains began thrusting upward. On the eastern edge of the Front Range, the horizontal sedimentary rocks located atop the Rampart Range Fault began doming. Slowly they tilted skyward and shattered.

Over the eons, the rocks most resistant to erosion became the towers, spires, and mushroom-shaped rocks of the Garden of the Gods, while the less resistant rocks eventually disappeared, the victims of wind and water.

area of only six square miles. The remains of the abandoned mines bunched together in clusters today give the impression of a prairie dog colony, once inhabited by enormous rodents.

The presence of precious minerals is the result of a major volcanic episode that manipulated the face of Colorado about 28 million years ago. The Rio Grande Rift, a major plate boundary that today stretches from central Mexico to Colorado, the culprit responsible for many of the massive earthquakes in Mexico recently, produced the lunar-like crater of the Cripple Creek diatreme.

The diatreme—a small nest of three circular volcanic basins—collapsed repeatedly during explosive episodes by draining continuing ejections of lava at the surface within the crater and by the subterranean release of molten magma to areas outside the Cripple Creek region. During the intervals between these pulsations of the diatreme, mineral-rich fluids began to move from great depths and seep into cracks, fissures, and faults where they cooled into the hard ore-bearing veins that the miners dreamed of finding.

Inside the crater today is a mishmash of rocks,

Pikes Peak amazonstone

Borrowing heavily from the diverse topography of the seven states it touches, Colorado is one of the most mineralized locales in the nation. Of all the precious stones, none is as characteristic of Colorado as Pikes Peak amazonstone.

Despite its tropical name, this crystalline feldspar has never been found anywhere near the Amazon. In the United States it is also found on the Eastern Seaboard, but Pikes Peak is the most productive area in the world for this gem.

Amazonstone occurs in pegmatites—coarse granite veins and pockets sprinkled with large interlocking crystals. In El Paso, Douglas, and Teller counties, these pegmatites are found cached in the reddish Pikes Peak granite. The amazonstone is usually associated with smoky quartz, rock crystal, topaz, fluorite, and mica.

Frequently termed "Pikes Peak jade" or "Colorado jade," the bright blue or green Pikes Peak amazonstone was first discovered in 1865. Eleven years later at its display debut at the Centennial Exposition in Philadelphia, this mineral turned the gem world on its ear.

Confident European exhibitors had laid in great quantities of amazonstone from the Ural Mountains in Russia, expecting exorbitant prices. Instead, the appearance of Pikes Peak amazonstone, which was superior in quality, quantity, and price, forced the unhappy speculators to remove the Russian variety from the market.

The choicest specimens in the world have come from the Crystal Peak area north of Florissant. Crystal Park, at the base of Cameron Cone, is also renowned for its amazonstone.

Amazonstone.
PHOTO BY WENDY SHATTIL/ ROBERT ROZINSKI, COURTESY DENVER MUSEUM OF NATURAL HISTORY

both volcanic and nonvolcanic in origin. The volcanic rocks are mainly latite, phonolite, syenite, and basalt, which formed when magma poured into vertical fractures and into the diatreme complex. The others are a combination of Precambrian granites and metamorphic rock and Oligocene fossil-bearing lake and stream deposits. All appear to have been shattered and reshattered during the continual wellings and collapses within the diatreme, bonding together differently in each interim finally to become the distinctive, mineral-rich host of Cripple Creek ore.

The nomenclature of Cripple Creek has been colored by both scientists and prospectors. The mass of angular rock fragments within the crater has been termed "breccia" by geologists, which simply means "broken" in Italian. To the early miners, the volcanic phonolite running in tubes throughout the breccia was known as "clink-stone" because it made a hollow pinging sound when tapped with a hammer.

And tap it with a hammer the miners did, hard and often. With some 500 mines operating there, employing 8,000 miners during the peak years, Cripple Creek was the place to be for those with dreams. Some got rich, some went broke, but they all helped to shape the history of Cripple Creek, just as the diatreme did 25 million years ago.

The Royal Gorge

It all looks fairly straightforward, peering down into the abyss of the Royal Gorge. The indomitable Arkansas River simply slashed through the ancient Precambrian granite, cutting deeper and deeper as time passed.

That is eventually what happened, but other forces, including some formidable block-faulting and an intriguing example of stream piracy, complicate what seems to be at first glance a textbook case of here-comes-the-river hydrology.

According to Sue Raabe, a Colorado Springs geologist who spent several years studying the Royal Gorge in pursuit of her doctoral degree, the spectacular chasm began to form 5 to 7 million years ago. About that time the Wet Mountains were undergoing renewed uplift to the south of the present gorge area. Immediately to the west of Canon City an enormous chunk of basement rock, measuring some 50 square miles, shifted along the

From the magnificent granite outcropping of Saint Peter's Dome, Gold Camp Road snakes its way to Cripple Creek. The most direct route from Colorado Springs to the gold camps during the mining heyday at the turn of the century, the rugged, 31-mile journey remains popular today. STEWART M. GREEN

Cathedral Spires, a mass of upheaved granite blocks along Gold Camp Road, have been rounded into turrets by constant weathering. STEWART M. GREEN

old fault lines bounding it and thrust its northeastern portion upward. A pair of streams consequently formed along joints in the crest of the block, one flowing northwest and the other southeast.

Gradually erosion deepened these streambeds until their heads came very close together, setting the stage for a geological phenomenon called stream piracy—the capture of one waterway by another. When this happens, the stream whose mouth empties into another body of water at a lower elevation than the other will become the pirating stream and will capture the other stream's drainage. In this case the southeasterly flowing stream

eventually captured the headwaters of the northwesterly flowing one, causing it to reverse its flow and change course by 180 degrees. This established the present-day direction of the Arkansas River through the Royal Gorge.

The combination of the newly formed river and a much wetter climate during the Pleistocene increased the volume of flow through the gorge. During storm-filled summer months, intense flash floods brought on by a combination of snow melt, glacial thawing, and heavy thunderstorms carried loads of debris and sediment through the deepening abyss.

Beneath the highest suspension bridge in the world, the Arkansas River flowing through the Royal Gorge has sliced through 1,053 feet of granite. TOM TILL

"Flash floods carry a great deal of sediment," Raabe said. "The Big Thompson flood [a disaster near Loveland, Colorado, in 1976 that killed 139 people] is a good example. The type of grinding action characteristic of these events has been observed to be responsible for the creation of deep gorges throughout North America.

"In the creation of the Royal Gorge, it does not seem to be a matter of slow, gradual erosion as much as a sporadic deepening when flooding occurred, followed by periods of normal flow and reduced erosion," she said. "Remember, we are talking in terms of millions of seasons as well as the melting of great volumes of ice during the interglacial periods."

The steep walls of the Royal Gorge are one of the calling cards of stream-cutting through hard granite and metamorphic rocks. Waterways that cut through softer, sedimentary rock tend to create broad, sloping valleys in humid regions and cliff-and-slope canyons like the Grand Canyon in drier climates.

Today, the deepest part of the Gorge, carved in rock laid down more than a billion years ago in primordial seas, is an obscure landmark marking the larcenous event. The result is one of the finest pieces of geological handiwork in all of Pikes Peak Country.

Florissant fossil beds

Thirty-six million years ago during the Oligocene, the shuddering Rio Grande Rift shook parts of the state like a rag doll. Crust-shattering earthquakes and volcanoes were the rule of the day for central and southwestern Colorado.

The climate in the Florissant Basin, 10 miles west of Pikes Peak, was moist, warm, and essentially semitropical. Deciduous and coniferous trees, lush ferns, insects, fish, birds, and mammals flourished. A major waterway ran through the basin to the south, a tributary of the ancient Arkansas drainage system which at that time flowed south from South Park, then eastward onto the Great Plains.

The sky was intermittently hazy as eruptions from ancient Mount Aetna in the Sawatch Range 50 miles west of Florissant poured enormous quantities of ash into the atmosphere and spilled heavy ashflows (a combination of ash, mud, and water) into the surrounding drainages and as far east as Pikes Peak and Castle Rock, Colorado.

About 34 million years ago, a volcano growing in the Thirtynine Mile Volcanic Field 17 miles west of the Florissant Basin began to erupt, spewing lava, mud, and ash into the area. Tremendous mudflows called lahars engulfed and destroyed the ancient forests in the Florissant valley; the stumps that remained were swamped by silicon-laden waters that eventually turned them to stone.

The river running through the area was blocked by the lahars and by the uplift of a broken wedge of basement rock at the south end of the present-day fossil beds termed the Hayden Divide. A large lake, Lake Florissant, formed in the entrapped basin.

Early estimates put its size at 12 miles by 2 miles; more recent information indicates that Lake Florissant may have been much larger, perhaps stretching another 10 miles or so into South Park.

Intense volcanic activity in the Thirtynine Mile Field continued over thousands of years, sweeping clouds of ash and dust eastward, trapping swarms of insects, and carrying plants into the lake, where they settled to the bottom. This produced alternating deposits of dust, ash, and lake sediments, entombing the ancient life in the impoundment.

Finally, with one tremendous thrust, the volcano exploded, forming the present-day Thirty-nine Mile Caldera. This deep caldera, the collapsed center of the volcano some 17 miles across with a circular wall of volcanic material, is visible just south of Elevenmile Reservoir. Tons of lava flowed northwest into South Park. To the northeast, the wall of the caldera gave way, sending the last of the lahars steadily rolling towards the Florissant Basin. Today, the remains of these lahars can be seen from the Fourmile Creek Road running east from Guffey, their imposing humps stopped as if by a camera.

The Florissant lake bed, which by this time had been reshaped by the volcano's constant barrage, was buried by these lahars, sealing millions of fossils under at least 45 feet of mud and rock.

Beginning about 12 million years ago, all of Colorado, including the Florissant Basin, was steadily uplifted nearly a mile in elevation. Although the rise increased in intensity about three million years ago, it would have been imperceptible to the human eye. Over the entire course of the lifting, the basin probably rose only inches a century. Corresponding to this uplift, the climate at Florissant became progressively more arid and much cooler.

Block-faulting during this time dropped the Florissant layers into their present valley setting, protecting them from erosion. Tons of debris, in the form of alluvial wash, were deposited in the basin in the ensuing Pleistocene ice ages. Following their termination some 7,000 years ago, the basin began warming and drying. The modern stream, Grape Creek, began the job of draining the Florissant Basin. This new waterway flows in the opposite direction of the Oligocene stream, however, and now runs north into the South Platte River drainage. Throughout the last 7,000 years, Grape Creek has done a remarkable thing. It has exposed the enormous petrified tree stumps as well as some of the fossil shales that form the unique focus of one of the world's most significant paleontological glimpses into the past.

Visitors are dwarfed by the petrified redwoods at Florissant Fossil Beds National Monument. STEWART M. GREEN.

The mushroom-shaped rocks of Red Canyon Park, north of Canon City, are similar to those in the Garden of the Gods. They illustrate the differential erosion that occurred throughout both parks over millions of years. STEWART M. GREEN

Monument Divide, also known as the Arkansas Divide, is the high point between Denver and Colorado Springs that cleaves the South Platte and Arkansas river drainages, sending the waters of the region on contrasting journeys. STEWART M. GREEN

The Cave of the Winds in Williams Canyon was sculpted into caverns and tunnels by underground rivers. The stalactites (from the ceiling) and the Stalagmites (from the floor) are believed to have been formed within the lst few thousand years by evaporating droplets of acidic groundwater seeping through limestone and leaving behind calcium carbonate. STEWART M. GREEN

Minarets, knobs, and huge boulders of red granite characterize the Lost Creek Wilderness Area at every corner. The weathering of these rocks has followed the joint planes, separating the boulders and rounding the sharp angles of their edges. STEWART M. GREEN

Massive granite formations in the Dome Rock area of Mueller State Park, southeast of florissant, dwarf a bighorn sheep.
WENDY SHATTIL

Above: On the plains near Calhan, east of Colorado Springs, gullies and arroyos have cut through sedimentary layers to form a series of badlands known as the Calhan Paint Mines. Once frequented by Cheyenne and Arapaho Indians, the Calhan area is paradoxical contrast to the verdure of much of Pikes Peak Country. MARK HEIFNER/THE STOCK BROKER

At left: The folds and cracks in the Pikes Peak granite of the Crags make it one of the most fascinating and heavily frequented areas for climbers in Colorado's Pikes Peak Country. MICHAEL S. SAMPLE

A summer thunderstorm batters the rolling grasslands of El Paso County near Colorado Springs. SPENCER SWANGER

*Granite and aspen dominate the
landscape near Rampart Reservoir
west of the U.S. Air Force Academy.
The reservoir lies on the eastern face
of the Rampart Range, a faulted
anticline running north from Colorado
Springs toward Castle Rock.*
STEWART M. GREEN

*Blooming May through July, the
pink-petaled wild rose is an important
food for pheasants, grouse, and
quail. The rose hips are eaten by
black bears in the fall. Ten species
of rose grow in the Rockies.*
MICHAEL S. SAMPLE

Of tsetse flies and stegosauruses

With its rolling meadows ringed by pine, spruce, fir, and aspen forests, the Florissant Basin today is an elegant place. Even the name is elegant. Florissant, in French, means blooming or flowering, which is exactly what the valley does each June and July when the wildflower extravaganza begins in earnest, blanketing the hillsides with Indian paintbrush, wild iris, blue columbine, and shooting stars.

At an elevation of 8,500 feet, the basin is also home to deer, elk, bighorn sheep, black bears, golden eagles, and mountain bluebirds, which graze, prowl, and soar in the shadow of Pikes Peak. The wildlife shares the astonishing Florissant landscape, compounding the sense of wildness.

Perhaps this was part of the attraction thousands of years ago, when Paleo-Indians used the Florissant Valley as a campground. Archaeologists have identified at least 20 sites dating back 8,000 years and marked by stone tools and flint flakes. Certainly the allure of the basin's natural features drew the homesteaders, who settled there beginning in the late 1860s. Today's visitors, however, are just as likely to come to observe Florissant's more subtle resources.

About 36 million years ago a catastrophic chain of events created the fossil beds of Florissant, which froze in time life from the Oligocene Epoch. Today, the Florissant Fossil Beds National Monument stands like a paleontological Pompeii.

No other site in the world boasts so many terrestrial species preserved from a single geologic period. Thanks in part to the shuddering of a restless volcano, nature's finest miniatures from ages ago lie encased in shale, a history stamped in stone.

Today an estimated 240,000 specimens

From rainbows to wildflowers, the charm of the Florissant basin goes far beyond its fossil treasures. MICHAEL S. SAMPLE

of fossil insects, plants, fish, birds, and mammals from the beds are on display in museums throughout the world. It is impossible to document, but at least that many Florissant fossils are tucked away in dens, garages, and attics, souvenirs collected over the last century by intrigued passers-by.

Among the scientific discoveries from Florissant are more than 1,100 varieties of insects, including ancient dragonflies, bees, spiders, beetles, aphids, and leafhoppers. Virtually all of the known butterflies in the New World as well as four species of the tsetse fly, which today are limited to tropical Africa, have been liberated from the delicate Florissant shales.

These relics are exquisite. Because of the fine consistency of the volcanic ash that captured the filmy carbon remains of these insects in paper-thin layers of shale, this ancient calligraphy is of stunning detail. Minute hairs from the legs of wasps are perfectly preserved, as are the intricate ribbings of termite wings. The fossils of butterflies have retained even the spots on their wings.

In addition to the insects, over 140 different plant species from the Oligocene Epoch, representing 44 modern families, have been identified from the beds. Some of the living relatives of these fossil plants exist today only in Africa, China, Australia, and South America. Though now composed of shale, the tiniest veins of the leaves are clearly visible, giving the impression that they were pressed yesterday from a backyard garden.

Insects and leaves are by far the most heralded specimens to come from the beds, but mollusks and vertebrates also contribute to the fossil record. The remains of ancient clams, carp-like fish, finches, and oreodonts (distant relatives of the modern pig) have been found embedded in the shales.

In contrast to the delicate fossils are the scores of enormous petrified tree stumps (more than 100 at last count). The largest of these, a sequoia measuring 14 feet tall and 74 feet in circumference, is thought to be biggest of its kind in the world, at one time standing an estimated 250 to 350 feet tall. Other tree stumps, notably cottonwood, ash, walnut, and poplar, also stand in stone there, complemented by the fossilized needles and leaves from birch, willow, maple, beech, hickory, and even palm and cypress trees. Some of these may have been blown into the volcanic debris from nearby highlands.

Looking at this evidence, scientists believe that the ancient climate at Florissant was nearly semitropical. Probably it was similar to the climate of northeastern Mexico today. Of the 91 species of fossil plants with living relations identified at Florissant, 69 of these are found today running in bands from southern Colorado to Chihuahua and from central Texas south to San Luis Potosi.

Early records show that the fossilized trees attracted most of the attention of the first settlers in Florissant and that the intricate fossils sealed in the shales were not noticed until some time later. Reportedly, Adam Hill, one of the first immigrants in the region, accidentally unearthed some of the fossils while trenching a series of steps outside his cabin door in the late 1860s.

The first scholarly look at the tiny fossils was taken by Theodore Mead, a young scientist from New York traveling through the region in 1871. While stopped at Station 39 (today known as Hartsel) on a butterfly-collecting excursion, he overheard word of the odd relics at Florissant. "I heard wonderful tales of

Standing in stone for 35 million years, a petrified redwood stump contrasts with the new growth of spring grass at Florissant Fossil Beds National Monument. MICHAEL S. SAMPLE.

petrified stumps and fossil insects 30 miles away," he wrote in his journal later, "so I hired a horse and went there, finding all as represented."

Because of his early and exhaustive work at Florissant, A.C. Peale, a field geologist for the U.S. Geological and Geographical Survey of the Territories, is credited with the first thorough investigation of the fossil beds in 1873. Astonished at what he found there after intensive excavation, Peale submitted a variety of plant and insect fossils for identification to the Swiss-born American paleontologist Leo Lesquereux, one of the premier scientists in the field of paleobotany in the United States at the time.

Lesquereux, along with paleontologists Edward Drinker Cope and Samuel Hubbard Scudder, made the first scientific evaluations of the Florissant fossil shales. Scudder was deeply impressed. Considered the founder of American insect paleontology, or paleoentomology, he arrived at Florissant in 1877, initiating a long relationship with the valley.

With the the help of several assistants, Scudder unearthed nearly 5,000 fossil specimens in just five days of work, a feat which made him ecstatic. "The extent of insect-bearing rocks which as yet have been touched only here and there," he wrote in an account of his first visit to the beds, "is so immensely greater than that of similar European strata that only lack of students in the field of American paleontology can prevent our deposits from assuring a commanding position in the world." His account, published in 1882 in a bulletin of the U.S. Geological Survey (the USGS was established by an act of Congress in 1879), was a glowing one in terms of the minute fossils; in terms of the petrified stumps, it was sobering. "Piecemeal they have been destroyed by vandal tourists, until not one of them rises more than a meter above the surface of the ground, and many of them are entirely leveled."

From its days of earliest discovery, the Florissant Basin has been irresistible to souvenir hunters. Although scientific exploration by institutions such as Colorado College and Princeton University accounted for the removal of wagonloads of fossils, tourists by the wagonload also stopped in and picked through the shales for keepsakes of their own.

As early as 1872, the idea that the paleontological treasures of Florissant were being despoiled was publicly recognized. That year, *Out West*, a popular magazine with a nationwide circulation, published a bleak prophesy. "One of the wonders of this part of the world is the 'Petrified Forest,' which is situated about halfway between Colorado Springs and Fairplay. This remarkable relic of former days, however, bids fair to disappear very shortly, unless the increasing crowd of tourists cease their work of destruction. Everyone must needs take a specimen, and some of the stumps are growing smaller at a very rapid rate."

Similarly, a reporter from the *Colorado Springs Gazette* made an observation in June 1890 that would later come back and haunt the region. "The expenditure of a few thousand dollars by the town of Florissant," he wrote, "in securing title to the land and digging out stumps and grading the grounds would make it a very great point of attraction for curiosity and pleasure seekers."

The suggestion went unheeded, however. In 1892 workers preparing for the World's Columbian Exposition in Chicago arrived at Florissant and began cutting four generous sections from the largest petrified stump in the world (known as "Big Stump"). Their efforts failed and several rusty blades still protrude from the stump, testimony to the folly of the operation.

The fossil beds remained a popular attraction as Florissant grew into a busy way station for the mining strikes in Cripple Creek, Leadville, Fairplay, Glenwood Springs, and Aspen. Following the arrival of the railroad in Florissant in 1887, it became the practice of the conductors to halt special excursion trains at the town, affording passengers the opportunity to hunt for fossils. For those too feeble or uninterested to look for relics on their own, local children were always on hand to sell them some.

Scientific evaluation of the fossil beds increased following Scudder's retirement in 1892. At the turn of the century, excavations by the American Museum in Washington, the University of Iowa, and the Denver Museum of Natural History and exhaustive work by T.D.A. Cockerell, an English entomologist, expanded Florissant's horizons considerably.

Cockerell, who came to Colorado in 1906 seeking relief from tuberculosis, found the fossils almost as much to his liking as the dry air and began studying with a frenzy. From his arrival in 1906 until 1935,

The making of the Florissant Fossil Bed

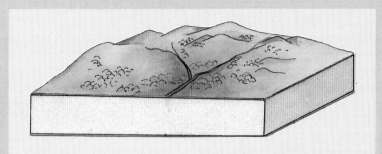

36 million years ago:
An ancient stream, fed by the moist, semitropical climate of Colorado at that time, flowed south through the Florissant Basin. The elevation, about 3,000 feet, was approximately a mile lower than it is today.

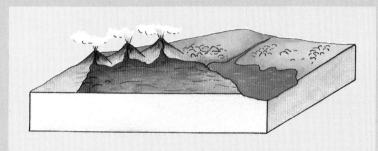

35 million years ago:
Eruptions in the Thirtynine Mine Volcanic Field 17 miles to the west sent lava, mud, and ash into the Florissant Basin, blocking stream drainage and forming a huge lake. A lush oasis for many life forms, Lake Florissant apparently existed for thousands of years.

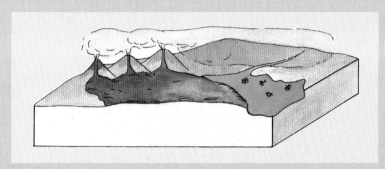

35 to 34 million years ago:
The Thirtynine Mile volcanoes erupted violently and repeatedly, spewing huge clouds of dust and ash over placid Lake Florissant. Thousands of life forms were trapped by the phenomena and eventually carried to the lake's bottom. This sediment formed the Florissant shales in which the fantastic fossils are found today.

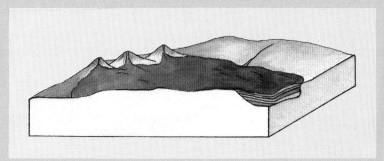

34 million years ago:
The Thirtynine Mile volcanoes continued to erupt. Thick mudflows known as lahars rolled in from the west, covering the lake and protecting the future shale beds. Among the fossils buried and preserved there are huge redwoods, magnolias, butterflies, beetles, and carp-like fish.

Between a rock and a hard place

Thirty-six million years ago many of the enormous trees at Florissant were buried in sediment, protected from the harsh weathering agents of wind, rain, and snow. By the turn of the last century, many of the petrified stumps had been excavated.

In recent years, however, some of these gigantic stone relics have been reburied. Park officials felt that they needed to be reinterred for their own protection.

Florissant naturalists have long been concerned about the natural weathering of these stumps, which splinter when frost causes ice wedges to form in the cracks of the petrified wood. But in this case, the stumps were reburied for another, all-too-human, reason.

Duncan Rollo, then Chief of Interpretation at Florissant, pointed to an ancient stump, now lying in pieces on the ground. Measuring about two feet across, the stump had been kicked apart by vandals in 1986.

"More than ninety-nine percent of our visitors are responsible people that are genuinely concerned with the preservation of this resource," Rollo said. "But this is the work of the other one percent."

As in any national park, vandalism is an ever-present threat. Earlier in the century, when it was still a commercial tourist haven, people took numbers of petrified wood relics from the Florissant beds. Some even hooked tow chains to the stumps and ripped them apart with their cars.

Overall, park visitors show a concern for preservation. During a recent case of fossilized wood theft, three different parties of tourists immediately reported the illegal activity to the visitor's center.

The solution to this dilemma lies in education, Rollo said. He takes pride in the fact that none of the employees of the national monument is a commissioned law enforcement officer. Instead, he said, they spend their time talking to the visitors. In addition to the standard interpretive programs, fully 50 percent of the people have some sort of personal contact with the rangers there.

"We can deal with the potential for vandalism through interpretive work," he said. "But when the federal budget gets strained, as it is now, the interpretive programs are one of the first things to go."

Rollo pointed out the spot where a 65-foot petrified log lay buried. "Do we dig it up?" he asked rhetorically. "It would make an incredible display, maybe one of the greatest things we could have here. We just haven't decided."

Deciding whether or not to trust park visitors is a difficult decision, a decison that affects preservation for the future. With 86 of the approximately 120 known petrified tree stumps at Florissant currently buried, the staff of the national monument is caught between a rock and a hard place.

Petrified redwood. MICHAEL S. SAMPLE

the University of Colorado professor published some 40 different papers on the fossil insects from the beds. In the process, he discovered the first fossil butterfly as well as the first tsetse fly.

His work was closely followed by that of Harry D. MacGinitie, a professor from the University of California at Berkeley, who initiated the most exhaustive study ever undertaken of the ancient plants of Florissant beginning in 1936. During the course of his work, MacGinitie not only refined the classification of 114 species of fossil plants uncovered there but also related their existence to the past climate, geology, evolution, and ecology of the basin.

In 1920 a group of interested scientists and other citizens made the first push to bring the Florissant treasures under the protective umbrella of the National Park Service. The idea received a brief local hearing, but no action was taken.

Six years later commercial development started in Florissant. P.J. "Red" Singer, who ranched the same land where Adam Hill first cut his steps and Scudder had done much of his work, opened a dude ranch, billing a portion of it as the "Colorado Petrified Forest." Singer openly welcomed scientific study of the fossils and hired guides to interpret the area for tourists. His attitude towards the fossil beds, that they were a treasure to be preserved, was shared by many of the local residents.

Singer's dude ranch proved to be a success. Up to 75 touring cars pulled in daily to see the fossil beds and petrified trees during the 1930s. This prompted Ivy Henderson to buy the land adjacent to Singer's and open his own resort under the name "Pike Petrified Forest."

In 1932 the question of protecting Florissant as a national park was raised again and dropped when Edmund Rogers, the superintendent of Yellowstone National Park, submitted an adverse report on its suitability, citing the large number of fossil forests nationwide and the facts that Florissant was privately owned, in no danger of being destroyed, and accessible to the general public.

By the 1940s tourists were becoming a nuisance, sneaking under the fences surrounding the private petrified forests (which both hosted small museums and tours) and taking away all that they could carry. Singer himself was especially concerned. Although he hoped the government would eventually assume management of the Colorado Petrified Forest, he

Granite boulders were deposited in the Florissant Basin by glaciers during the ice age. MICHAEL S. SAMPLE

wondered if the increasing vandalism and theft at the fossil beds might soon make it too late to save them.

In 1952 attempts to have the area designated as a national park were again rebuffed. The National Park Service finally recommended in 1962 that the area be preserved.

But legislation to establish the park failed in Congress in 1963, 1965, and again in 1967. By the spring of 1969, while yet another Florissant bill was laboring in Congress, the threat of land development atop the fossil beds had become a very real possibility.

A group of scientists and concerned citizens formed a group called the "Defenders of Florissant, Inc.,"

Generally speaking, fossils are evidence of prehistoric life. The intricate insect and plant fossils at Florissant resulted from carbonization, a process that preserves the organisms as films of carbon, which highlight the structure of the specimens exquisitely but one-dimensionally. The antennae of ancient wasps, the delicate veins of prehistoric leaves—even minute pollen grains which can be plainly viewed under a microscope—are all examples of carbonization's work in the Florissant Fossil Beds.

Top left: A wasp preserved at Florissant Fossil Beds National Monument. LEO L. LARSON

Middle left: A beetle from the Oligocene Epoch is part of the fossil record at Florissant. WENDY SHATTIL

Bottom left: An ancient ant ensnared by volcanic ash from the Thirtynine Mile Volcano Field some 36 million years ago, was carried to the bottom of Lake Florissant. WENDY SHATTIL

Top right: Oligocene Epoch plant life such as this specimen, indicates that warmer, semitropical climatic conditions prevailed at Florissant 36 million years ago. LEO L. LARSON

Bottom right: A crane fly from the Florissant Fossil Beds National Monument, is preserved in intricate detail, the ribbing on its wings still visible. WENDY SHATTIL

The sharp summit of McIntyre Mountain, southeast of Castle Mountain. The two peaks are located just east of the Thirty-nine Mile Caldera, whose volcanic activity was in part responsible for the intricate fossils at Florissant. STEWART M. GREEN

The rose-purple petals of shooting stars blanket the Florissant region through portions of each summer. The genus name, Dodecatheon, *means "twelve gods"—suggesting that the flower resembles a group of gods or is under the care of a dozen deities.* MICHAEL S. SAMPLE

aimed at protecting the land and its treasures. After initiating a letter-writing campaign to senators and representatives, some of the committee members journeyed to Washington to testify at a hearing on behalf of the proposed national monument bill.

One Defender, Beatrice Willard, a University of Colorado professor and the president of the Colorado Open Space Council, highlighted the fossils that make Florissant unique in her Congressional testimony. The resource, she eloquently concluded, "makes the Florissant beds comparable in the record of life to the Dead Sea Scrolls of Biblical fame, the Rosetta Stone that unlocked the secrets of ancient Egyptian civilization, and the Gutenberg

Bible that recorded the first Western printing."

The bill proposing Florissant as a national monument subsequently passed in the Senate, but it was still bogged down in a House committee in late June. With bulldozers from the Colorado Springs area now creeping up Ute Pass and the development of the area seemingly imminent, the ad-hoc group attempted to buy time by filing suit in the U.S. District Court in Denver on July 3, seeking an injunction against development. The injunction was denied on July 9.

With that, Defender Roger Hansen, executive director of the Rocky Mountain Center for the Environment, flew to Washington to meet with U.S. Supreme Court Justice Byron White.

White, although sympathetic, directed the Defenders to first exhaust all of their remedies in the lower courts. The following day, an emergency motion was put before a three-judge panel of the U.S. Tenth Circuit Court of Appeals in Denver.

There was no direct statutory protection for fossils. "What right have we to control the use of private land unless there is a nuisance perpetrated by the owners?" Chief Judge Jean S. Breitenstein asked Victor Yannacone, Jr., one of the Defenders' lawyers.

"Your honor," Yannacone answered, "If someone had found the original United States Constitution buried on his land, and wanted to use it to mop up a stain on the floor, is there any doubt that he could be prevented?"

A restraining order was granted that day. The bulldozers surrounding Florissant, which were literally idling from time to time, were temporarily silenced. Following a return to the District Court on July 29 (where the injunction was again denied), the Defenders of Florissant returned to the Circuit Court of Appeals and obtained yet another restraining order the next day.

A week later the House passed legislation providing for a 6,000-acre national monument at a cost of $3,727,000. On August 20, 1969, President Richard M. Nixon signed the bill to establish Florissant Fossil Beds National Monument.

The court case was a landmark. For the first time, the courts protected a unique natural resource at the expense of private property ownership. Perhaps more important, it also marked the first time that fossils were legally considered a natural resource.

Since its establishment, Florissant Fossil Beds National Monument has become a popular place indeed. During its first year of operation, 9,000 people visited. Today, about 90,000 people visit Florissant annually.

What's the attraction? Florissant's magnetism is directly attributable to its fossils, but the other natural resources there, notably the wildlife, wildflowers, cultural history, and geologic features, also contribute to the allure.

At Florissant nature provides an incredible wildflower extravaganza, and the show can change almost daily. During the summer months, park naturalists help identify and explain not only the floral display but the fossil record as well. For more adventurous tourists, day-long field seminars covering geology, wildlife, and wildflowers are also offered.

One of the most popular activities at Florissant in recent years has been the "Night Hikes." Visitors confront the secluded valley in total darkness, relying on their own sensory perceptions to eavesdrop on the nocturnal residents of the park, which include owls, coyotes, bobcats, and bats.

During the winter months, public activities focus on the nine miles of cross-country ski trails. Visitors can also stroll through the park on snowshoes checked out from the visitor's center. A variety of winter ecology programs are offered, including animal-tracking seminars.

Another feature is the 160-acre Hornbek Homestead, a century-old farm at the north end of the monument, which was restored during the nation's bicentennial celebration. Here tourists learn about the harsh life settlers like Adeline Hornbek and her three children led. Today, the original cabin, as well as reconstructed barns, a carriage shed, a bunkhouse, and root cellar recall an earlier way of life.

Thirty-five miles south of Florissant, on the southern boundary of Pikes Peak Country, lies Canon City—a paleontological hotbed in its own right. This area lacks the rumbling volcanic history and plant and insect remains that are the hallmark of Florissant, but its fossil record is every bit as formidable.

The ride north out of Canon City, up the Fourmile Creek Road to its eventual meeting with the bone-jarring Shelf Road, is a journey through time. Although the actual distance covered to the junction of the Shelf Road overlooking Helena Canyon is less than 10 miles, travelers can look back more than a billion years through geologic history.

The rocks exposed on the left side of the highway tell the story. Lying diagonally in distinct layers, the flayed segments of rock expose the past like the pages of a book. At the bottom of the jumble are the ancient Precambrian rocks, entombed in a basement of granite. Next, neatly deposited on their backs, sandstone layers from the Ordovician period testify to the age-old oceans that once covered Colorado.

Locked in this sandstone are tiny blue specks, often missed by the casual observer. To paleontologists, however, they are enormously significant. A century ago the dots were identified as tiny fossilized platelets of Agnathid fishes that flourished in Colorado some 500 million years ago. Today they are considered to

The Cope-Marsh feud

This is the story of two eminent scientists, the gigantic dinosaur skeletons they raced to uncover, and their bitter feud.

Edward Drinker Cope, a Philadelphia paleontologist, and Othniel Charles Marsh, a Yale University professor, were the most prolific dinosaur discoverers of the nineteenth century. When they began their careers, nine different species of dinosaurs were known from North American sites. By the time they were finished, 136 more had been uncovered.

Initially, Cope and Marsh were friends. Cope even went so far as to name a fossil for his colleague—*Pytonius marshii*. But the increasing frequency of dinosaur discoveries and the advent of the railroads to the West raised the stakes in vertebrate paleontology. Competition between the two scientists turned into fierce rivalry.

Cope, left, Marsh, right.
PHOTOS COURTESY DENVER PUBLIC LIBRARY, WESTERN HISTORY DEPARTMENT

Since the road to scientific immortality is the naming of new species, Cope and Marsh fought hard in the contest for nomenclature. In 1872 Marsh was working in the Bridger Basin in southwestern Wyoming. He was angered when Cope showed up uninvited and began excavations of his own several valleys over. When Cope rushed to a remote railroad outpost to wire word east of significant paleontological finds, Marsh considered this claim-jumping and the feud was on.

In 1877, dubbed "the Year of the Dinosaur" because of the number and magnitude of discoveries, the fires were fanned once again. It began early in March with the discovery of a significant dinosaur quarry near Morrison, Colorado. Although Cope managed to secure the first bones from the site, Marsh was awarded control of the quarry by the landowner, an event that stunned Professor Cope.

Incredibly, that same month the tables turned. An even more important discovery occurred at Garden Park. Schoolmaster O.W. Lucas of Canon City alerted Cope first. Because of the larger and more complete skeletons at Garden Park, it was now Marsh's turn to fret. But not for long. He soon dispatched his own diggers to the Garden Park area.

The next round went to Marsh. In July he got word of an even more staggering find at Como Bluff in Wyoming, which eventually became the greatest dinosaur graveyard yet discovered. By some estimates, the boneyard stretched seven miles. Cope was left in the dust once again.

The feud intensified throughout the 1880s. The two men attacked each other in scientific journals, a practice their colleagues found tiresome. Cope sarcastically referred to his rival as "the Professor of Copeology at Yale." Marsh referred to Cope simply as that "damned thief."

Both continued work into the 1890s, with Marsh having greater success. Cope lost a fortune in sour mining investments and was forced to curtail much of his field work. Cope died in 1897, Marsh two years later. The feud was finally over.

be among the oldest known relics of vertebrate life in the world.

For fossil fans, the Canon City region is a motherlode. Just a few miles south of the tiny fish fossils on the Fourmile Creek Road lie some of Colorado's greatest paleontological treasures. The location is Garden Park, eight miles north of Canon City, which in its heyday was one of the most talked-about dinosaur graveyards in the world.

The story begins on a spring-like March day in 1877. O.W. Lucas, the superintendent of schools for Fremont County, was roaming the hills near Garden Park. Marveling at the flora, he stumbled upon several enormous fossil fragments protruding from a bed of shale. Among Lucas' finds was a fossilized femur (upper leg bone) five feet long.

Being of the scientific persuasion himself as an amateur botanist, Lucas knew about the work of Professor Edward D. Cope, the eminent paleontologist from Philadelphia. Cope, along with Othniel C. Marsh, another well-known paleontologist, had been making highly publicized dinosaur discoveries. So Lucas sent off a sampling of bone fragments to Cope for identification.

One vertebrate section particularly excited Cope, who announced that it "exceeds in proportions any other land animal hitherto described...." Cope dubbed the dinosaur *Camarasaurus* (a member of the gigantic sauropod dinosaurs) and named Lucas and his brother Ira as directors of the Canon City dig.

The Garden Park Quarry became an important site because of its completeness. Although restricted to a band measuring only about three feet thick, its shale eventually added some 28 species and genera to the taxonomy of vertebrate paleontology.

The discovery quickly turned into a free-for-all. Although Cope had the best location at first, Marsh quickly moved quarriers of his own into nearby shale deposits. Some of the largest and most complete dinosaur skeletons ever discovered were exhumed from the Garden Park region, and excavations continued on sporadically into 1930.

Now Garden Park dinosaurs are scattered across the country. In Washington, D.C., a tyrannosaurus skeleton stands at the American Museum, a diplodicus rests in the Carnegie Musuem, and a ceratosaurus adorns the U.S. National Museum. Elsewhere, stegosaurus skeletons grace both the Denver Museum of Natural History and the Yale Peabody Museum; a brontosaurus sits in the Philadelphia Academy of Science, and a haplocarthosaurus guards the Cleveland Museum of Natural History.

Two major contributions to paleontology were made at Garden Park. First was its fantastic collection of dinosaur skeletons from 150 million years ago. Second was the novel method developed by excavators there for preserving and transporting bones from the quarries to the laboratory. They wrapped them in cloth and plaster of Paris—a method that is still widely used in paleontology today.

From the enormous dinosaurs that lumbered through Garden Park to the minute tsetse flies that buzzed over the Florissant Basin, life in the Pikes Peak region has been evolving for millions of years. Today, thanks to a series of geological quirks and the tireless digging of a few dedicated paleontologists, we can look back as if it were yesterday.

Normally found growing in damp soil, this cinquefoil, commonly called yellow rose, has taken root in a crack, where it will continue to wedge this Pikes Peak granite apart. Though not preferring it, big game will eat cinquefoil. Because it keeps its leaves in the winter, it furnishes nourishment during the critical months.
STEWART M. GREEN

Pollen cones, ponderosa pine, above. At flowering time, the pollen is released, carried on the wind to female ponderosa conelets. W. PERRY CONWAY

Opportunistic coyotes, left, share the Florissant region with hundreds of wildlife and wildflower species. Despite man's best efforts to eradicate these canids during the settling of the West—through poisoning, trapping, and shooting—coyotes are probably more common now than they ever were. Their prolific litter sizes of 5 to 6 pups and habit of eating almost anything are in part responsible for their evolutionary success. MICHAEL S. SAMPLE

A never-ending procession

Just as the Pikes Peak region's geologic and fossil record is cast in stone, so, too, is its earliest historical evidence. Crude stone tools, chipped, flaked, and wielded by Archaic Indians some 8,000 years ago, indicate the presence of a hunting and gathering culture. Washed through sandy arroyos and down steep ravines over the ages, these ancient relics provide a lithic legacy all their own.

How much further back might this archaeological record go? According to experts, the Front Range of Colorado was the first place in the New World where mammoth bones were discovered in association with man. With these finds dating back 12,000 years, who knows when the first Paleo-Indians (whose ancestors may have slogged across the Bering Land Bridge as early as 15,000—20,000 years ago) arrived in Pikes Peak Country?

Indians are known to have inhabited the Pikes Peak region for nearly 2,000 years before the first explorers arrived. The historical tribes included the Utes, who were entrenched by the 1700s not only in their rock forts along Fountain Creek on the Ute Pass trail, but also throughout Colorado's central Rocky Mountains.

The acquisition of the horse by many of the West's Indian cultures during the eighteenth century spelled mobility. The Comanches and Kiowas as well as the Cheyennes and Arapahos formed alliances on the Great Plains and frequently ventured into the mountains in pursuit of big game.

The Spanish, too, knew the Pikes Peak region, as Zebulon Pike extolled in his journal: "Indeed it was so remarkable as to be known by all the savage nations for hundreds of miles around, and to be

Staggering sunsets, like the one above, were a common sight to the early travelers in quest of the Rocky Mountain goldfields. By December of 1858, at least three separate guidebooks detailing the location and resources of the Pikes Peak region were off the presses and available to travelers heading out from the East and Midwest. STEPHEN TRIMBLE

Visible for more than 100 miles across the eastern plains, Pikes Peak has always been the landmark of travelers. Pike first spotted the great mountain from a point near Holly, Colorado, near the Kansas border. In this view, looking to the south from the Rampart Range, the peak juts into the plains.
STEWART M. GREEN

spoken of with great admiration by the Spaniards of N. Mexico and was the bounds of their travels N.W."

The earliest trappers and mountain men trickled in and out of the region. A French trapper named Bourgement, while plying his trade in beaver-rich South Park, reported the presence of Comanches there in 1723. In Santa Fe in 1806 Pike himself met up with mountain man James Pursley, who boasted of having found gold in South Park several years before.

It was Pike, of course, whose surname captured the countryside. Despite his failed attempt at scaling the tall mountain, which he referred to both as "Grand Peak" and "Blue Peak," the young lieutenant provided Americans a heady vision. His 1806 expedition, although at times bordering on folly, was nevertheless an extremely valiant one. He and his 15 men, alone in an unmapped wilderness, managed to discover the headwaters of the South Platte and Arkansas rivers as well as the Royal Gorge, enduring considerable hardship in the process.

The Pike expedition in Colorado was a haphazard one. After he was repelled by the snows and icy temperatures on the peak in late November, the party veered south and followed the Arkansas River

upstream to the Royal Gorge. Blocked by the narrow canyon, the men turned north up Fourmile Creek, eventually making their way to the South Platte River near the mouth of Elevenmile Canyon. Continuing northwest, they traversed much of South Park, turned back southwest in mid-December, and camped near present-day Buena Vista.

After spending a cheerless Christmas in the Salida area, Pike and his men began following the Arkansas River (which they mistook for the long sought-after Red River) downstream. This jagged circle they traveled brought them back to their original campsite at Canon City a month later.

"We were lost," lamented the lieutenant, "and thought we were on the Red River." He resigned himself to his journal and wrote morosely of his twenty-seventh year. "This was my birthday, and most fervently did I hope never to pass another so miserably."

After building a stockade at their original campground near the Canon City site, the expedition was forced to leave behind several members who were suffering from severely frozen feet. The party, now 11 men, proceeded south on Grape Creek to the Wet Mountain Valley and over the Sangre de Cristo

Mountains to the site of present-day Alamosa. Here a battalion of more than 100 Spaniards intercepted them, escorting Pike and his men under armed guard to Santa Fe.

Pike was subsequently taken to Chihuahua, Mexico, interrogated, and released at the Texas border. In the process, all of his papers were confiscated. Although the men he had left behind were later rescued by the Spanish, Pike's demeaning arrest long overshadowed his genuine exploratory feats.

The Stephen Long expedition of 1819 to 1820, a party of 22 men dispatched West on essentially the same mission as Pike's, explored the Front Range of Colorado from the Poudre River to the Arkansas. This group had an easier time. It was mid-summer, instead of the dead of winter. Criticized in some quarters back East for failing to locate the headwaters of the Red River, the Long party is today remembered best for two things. Foremost was the first recorded ascent of Pikes Peak by Dr. Edwin James, the botanist and surgeon who accompanied the party. Second was James' dismal assessment of the region, which he dubbed "the Great American Desert." Part of his report claimed the aridity of the West was "serving as a barrier to prevent expansion of our population westward." Antiexpansionist politicians in Washington, including the silver-tongued Daniel Webster, quoted James' conclusions widely during Congressional hearings.

Colonel Henry Dodge and his 117 U.S. Army Dragoons, assigned to improve relations with the western Indian tribes, traveled through the Pikes Peak region in 1835. Seven years later, John Charles Fremont and his railroad survey passed through. Despite the fact that Long had named the massive mountain in honor of James in 1820, both Dodge and Fremont referred to it as "Pike's Peak" on their maps, assuring Zebulon a prominent place in history.

The "Fontaine que Bouille"—the boiling springs at the base of Pikes Peak, the site of the present-day Manitou Springs—was nearly as much a landmark in the area as the mountain itself. In 1846 Lieutenant George Frederick Ruxton, an Englishman who traveled extensively through the West and wrote authoritatively about the mountain life, visited the renowned spa. At the bottom of the clear pools, he was astounded to see beads, knives, and wampum strewn about, as if in a wishing well.

"The Indians regard with awe the 'medicine' waters of these fountains, as being the abode of a spirit who breathes through the transparent water," he later wrote in *Adventures in Mexico and the Rocky Mountains*, "thus, by his exhalations, causes the perturbation of its surface."

Although much of the ballyhooed "Pikes Peak or Bust" gold rush of 1859 initially bypassed the region for points north, gold strikes in South Park—most notably on the Blue River near Hoosier Pass and on Tarryall Creek near Como—caused a flurry of activity. That year, a party of prospectors from Kansas staked out a town they named El Dorado at the base of the Ute Pass trail, anticipating an exodus to the goldfields.

Later renamed Colorado City, the settlement carved a temporary niche for itself on the coattails of South Park diggings. Of the estimated 48,000 Americans in Colorado territory in 1860, 11,000 of them were scraping through the streams of the huge park, searching for their fortunes.

Colorado City took full advantage of its strategic location, advertising its highway to South Park as well as its natural wonders and medicinal waters. For a brief period it flourished, even becoming the territorial capital of Colorado from the autumn of 1861 through the summer of 1862, when Denver began emerging as the region's commercial and political center.

The Civil War, though states away, spelled trouble for Colorado City. Westward expansion of the United States slowed to a crawl along the southern Arkansas route, while the northern passage along the North Platte became more popular. Finally, the South Park rush, like most gold booms, slowly played out, leaving Colorado City to wallow in its own dust.

Tumble-down shacks were what General William J. Palmer saw when he alighted from a stagecoach at Colorado City in 1869. But the flamboyant promoter of the Denver and Rio Grande Railroad knew that first appearances could be deceiving. A man of professional vision, he looked past the dying town to the great peak, the bubbling springs, and the Garden of the Gods. And he formed a plan.

"My theory for this place," he wrote, "is that it should be made the most attractive place in the West for homes—a place for schools, colleges, literature, science, first-class newspapers, and everything the above implies." In short order a city was born.

A singular man

Dr. Edwin James died in Burlington, Iowa, in 1861 at the age of 63. His passing for the most part went unnoticed. His neighbors considered him affable enough but eccentric, a man who kept to himself.

"It did not take me long to discover that it was not for me to make my mark upon the age," he wrote later. "I will rule my own spirit, and thus be greater than he who taketh the city."

Contrary to his own perception, James indeed made a name for himself. When he entered the Pikes Peak region as a 22-year-old surgeon and botanist with the Long Expedition in 1820, it was a wild and unexplored country. After his return, America knew it much better.

James became the first man to scale the 14,110-foot peak, today one of the nation's most famous mountains. By becoming the first botanist to collect alpine flora from the tundra of North America (which he did during his climb, later describing and naming some 20 plants), he made July 14, 1820, the date of his ascent, one of the great days in the history of botanical collections.

A principled man of varied interests and actions, James wrote the official Long Expedition report for the U.S. government. He also transcribed one of the best and earliest accounts of the tribal relations of American Indians, detailing the intricacies of the Ojibway tongue. During the Civil War he conducted an underground railroad from his home in Iowa to Illinois for blacks.

Today, blue columbines, which he first described near Palmer Lake and which later became Colorado's state flower, bloom on his grave each year in Iowa, far from the Southern Rocky Mountains. His name now graces 13,260-foot James Peak, which towers over the Moffat Tunnel near Berthoud Pass. And though his name was removed from the greatest peak, discarded in favor of Pike's after 14 years, his independent, adventurous spirit continues to permeate Pikes Peak Country.

Colorado blue columbine, Aquilegia coerulea. STEWART M. GREEN

First assigned the name of the Fountain Colony, the community was secured by Palmer's purchase of 10,000 acres of land surrounding the confluence of Fountain Creek and Monument Creek at 80 cents per acre. Palmer then turned around and resold it to the Colorado Springs Company, his newly formed development enterprise, for $15 an acre. Three months later, by no great coincidence, the tracks of the Denver and Rio Grande Western Railroad arrived in town.

The true keys to the city, in this case, were Palmer's Iron Horses. He knew from experience that by developing towns he could pay for the railroads, so he advertised rail travel to the community in newspapers and magazines, plugging it as a scenic wonderland and health resort.

In the shadow of the peak and beside the mineral springs came hotels, schools, churches, and courtrooms. In 1874 Colorado College and the Colorado School for the Deaf and Blind were constructed on Colorado Springs Company land. At the urging of local physicians who claimed that the climate there offered perhaps the world's best therapeutic environment for the treatment of tuberculosis, sanitoriums soon followed.

The town, located adjacent to the original Colorado City, soon adopted the name of Colorado Springs. To many, however, it was better known as "Little London." Palmer's circle of friends included quite a few Englishmen, who, in addition to afternoon tea, introduced sports like fox hunting, cricket, golf, and polo to a city that had been nothing but a hard-bitten prospector's dive two decades earlier.

To the southeast, Canon City, born in 1860 as a sister supply camp to the South Park goldfields, was undergoing its own awakening. In 1868, when offered a choice by the territorial government of hosting either the state's penitentiary or university, Canon City officials opted for the former, apparently preferring compulsory attendance at their new facility.

The railroad arrived in Canon City in 1874. Four years later a highly publicized railroad war between the Denver and Rio Grande line (Palmer's company) and the Atchison, Topeka, and Santa Fe company over the right-of-way

Battle of Bayou Salado

In the spring of 1852 legendary mountain man Kit Carson, along with William Drannan and Johnnie West, camped in South Park to hunt beaver. Carson met up with an old acquaintance, Chief Kiwatchee of the Comanche tribe. Kiwatchee related to Carson that the Comanches were readying for a battle with the Utes over hunting privileges, a contest they had arranged by mutual agreement. Although Carson declined the chief's invitation to participate, he and his friends postponed their departure in order to observe the confrontation.

The warriors and their families arrived at the battle site (possibly at Cross Creek) in early May. After days of preparation, they squared off; the Comanches on the south side of the creek and the Utes on the north.

"They fought hard all day," Drannan wrote later. "Sometimes the Comanches would cross over to the same side with the Utes, and I saw many hand-to-hand fights with tomahawks and knives." The night "was made hideous by the shrieks and cries of the squaws and children of warriors." The second day and night repeated the first. On the third and last day, the Comanches killed several dozen Ute warriors in the morning. That afternoon Chief Kiwatchee's men charged, driving the Utes to the top of a nearby knoll and forcing them to cross the prearranged boundary that marked the end of the battle. The Comanches paraded victoriously back across the creek with 100 of the Ute's horses. More important, they had won the hunting rights to South Park, at least until the next challenge.

through the Royal Gorge began. The brouhaha over the tracks, intended to serve the burgeoning silver camps at Leadville, climaxed with the construction of armed forts on both sides of the canyon. It ended without a shot being fired, however, as the U.S. Supreme Court granted the Denver and Rio Grande the right of way.

In addition the Midland Railroad from Colorado Springs plowed west over Ute Pass in 1887 in response to the mineral bonanzas in Leadville, Aspen, and Glenwood Springs, nurturing the blossoming settlements of Woodland Park, Divide, Florissant, and Lake George along the way.

On Pikes Peak itself, tracks were reaching skyward. In 1890 construction of a cog railroad was begun and was completed the following year. The railway, with a vertical climb of 7,158 feet over nine miles and a 16 percent grade, was modeled after a similar system in the Swiss Alps.

In 1891 a second wave of gold fever hit the Cripple Creek basin. The most important event in the history of Pikes Peak Country, it began with the discovery in late 1890 of a rich vein by cowboy Bob Womack, followed in short order by scores of other strikes. By 1900 there were 55,000 people living in the region (25,000 in Cripple Creek alone), with 11 towns crammed in the six-square-mile area.

In its heyday the district boasted 15 newspapers, 90 doctors, and every conceivable enterprise from dance schools to business colleges. A total of 150 saloons threw their doors open, most of them located on infamous Myers Avenue in Cripple Creek. This gaiety was offset somewhat by the 34 churches in the district that served a more sober-minded populace.

Recreations like horseracing, rodeos, circuses, skating, professional baseball, and operas were widely enjoyed, and even such notable heavyweight prizefighters as Jack Johnson and Jack Dempsey (who moonlighted in the Portland Mine as a mucker—a worker who clears debris from the tunnels and shafts) fought there.

Pinnacle Park, erected just west of the town of Cameron, was a popular diversion. With an electric merry-go-round, motion pictures, shooting galleries, zoo, dancing pavilion, baseball field, saloons, dining halls, and vaudeville acts, it attracted thousands of people nightly.

Pikes Peak or Bust!

During the Pikes Peak gold rush of 1858, hordes of fortune seekers intent on the goldfields of the Colorado Territory rolled westward in Conestoga wagons. As many as 100,000 people from the eastern states set out for Colorado during the spring of that year, and approximately half of them eventually reached their destination.

Perhaps the most common sport in the district was "high-grading." This pastime consisted of stealing high-grade ore from the mines and secreting it in one's clothes, hats, pockets, and even more inventive places. Although this larceny was eventually curbed with the introduction of closely guarded dressing rooms at the mines, profits from this multimillion-dollar-a-year enterprise were used by miners to pay everybody from the parson to the prostitute.

During this glorious time all roads led to Cripple Creek. The first train to reach the goldfields was the Florence and Cripple Creek Railroad, also known as the Gold Belt Line, which began running three passenger trains a day up Phantom Canyon in 1894. A year later the Midland Terminal Railroad, which ran from Colorado Springs to the Aspen and Leadville mining camps, started a spur line at Divide running south through Gillette, Cameron, and Victor. In 1899 the Short Line, the most direct and scenic route to the region, began operation across the east and south slopes of Pikes Peak. Even an interurban electric trolley system was installed in the Cripple Creek district, allowing residents to travel virtually anywhere at a nickel a ride.

In 1900 more than $18 million in gold was mined from the Cripple Creek district. At the Portland Mine in Victor, the largest mine in the region, some 700 men were employed, working round-the-clock shifts. At the Cresson Mine between Cripple Creek and Victor, the lode was so rich that armed guards escorted the ore, which was securely locked in boxcars, all the way to Colorado Springs.

Several great fires swept Victor and Cripple Creek, but the towns barely missed a step. In 1896 two enormous blazes in a five-day period virtually leveled Cripple Creek, causing $2 million in damage and leaving 5,000 homeless. Three years later Victor underwent a similar fate when a fire destroyed 12 blocks and 200 buildings. In a matter of days the rebuilding process was begun in both cities—this time with brick.

In 1903 a period of labor strife hammered the Cripple Creek District. It began when mine owners brought in scabs to work following a union strike involving demands for higher wages and better working conditions. On July 6, 1904, a railroad platform in Independence (a mile and a half north

A Pikes Peak poet

Colorado Springs, wrote Helen Hunt Jackson, is "a town lying due east of the great mountains and west of the sun."

Called "the greatest poet in America" by Ralph Waldo Emerson, Jackson came to Colorado Springs in 1873 from New England, seeking relief from severe bronchial problems. Although she married prominent local banker William Sharpless Jackson in 1875, she avoided high society and instead spent her time admiring the stunning beauty of the surrounding area. While living in Colorado Springs, she wrote seven books and a wide array of articles and poems, many of which reflected the natural resources unique to Pikes Peak Country.

In 1879 she left for the Eastern Seaboard to embark on her efforts to improve the lot of American Indians. In 1881 she published *A Century of Dishonor*, an historical account of the government's injustice in its treatment of Indians.

As a result, she obtained a Congressional appointment as a special commissioner to investigate the conditions of the Mission Indians of southern California. This experience led her to write *Ramona*, a tragic novel about the life of a Mission Indian girl. The work strongly stated her indictment of U.S. Indian policy and ultimately won her the greatest acclaim of her career.

Jackson returned to Colorado Springs briefly in 1884. She died the following year in California.

Helen Hunt. PHOTO COURTESY DENVER PUBLIC LIBRARY WESTERN HISTORY DEPARTMENT

Best remembered for her literary works on behalf of Native Americans, she is also revered in the Pikes Peak region for her eloquent portrayals of its simple yet breathtaking panoramas.

---

of Victor) loaded with nonunion workers was blown up, killing 13 and seriously injuring more than a dozen others. Rioting between union and nonunion factions followed in Cripple Creek and Victor, and the state militia, acting under martial law, herded hundreds of union miners into bullpens before deporting them from the region. The labor strife lasted 18 months, the nonunion forces finally prevailing.

After 1900 as the ore resources began to dwindle, the glory days of Cripple Creek started to lose their luster. By 1920 only 40 of the original 500 mines were in operation. Colorado Springs tycoons, who had invested heavily in the goldfields, had made

their fortunes, however. Between 1900 and 1910 that municipality was the richest city per capita in the United States, with one-twentieth of the state's population clutching one-fourth of the state's bank deposits.

One of the richest residents was Spencer Penrose, an immigrant from Pennsylvania who made his millions at Cripple Creek. Shortly after he bank-rolled the Pikes Peak Toll Road in 1916, he set out to resurrect the Broadmoor.

The original Broadmoor Casino, built in 1891, flourished briefly before burning to the ground in 1897. A reconstructed version of it failed financially shortly thereafter, but Penrose stepped in during

"What's going on up there?"

The U.S. Signal Service Station, constructed in 1873 atop Pikes Peak as a weather station, was a strange place.

The first two inhabitants of the meteorological outpost are said to have met grim fates. Just before Christmas 1873 a sergeant reportedly died mysteriously at the top and was buried in an unmarked grave. The other man, a corporal, was a blathering idiot by the time he was rescued. He spent the remainder of his life in an asylum.

Probably the most famous inhabitant of the top was John O'Keefe, a member of the U.S. Signal Corps who began gathering weather data on the peak in 1876. Were it not for his acquaintance with Judge Eliphalet Price (a justice of the peace turned reporter who first met O'Keefe when sentencing him to jail for fighting), the signal station employee might never have gained the fame that he did.

Following their curious introduction, the pair became fast friends, sharing the same passion for saloons and storytelling. After Price's switch to a journalism career, they began hatching outlandish stories by barlight, which Price would transform into "news releases." One such story dealt with alleged sea monsters inhabiting a lake near Pikes Peak, another with a purported volcanic eruption of the mountain.

Price and O'Keefe's most famous caper came in 1877 when they collaborated on a story about man-eating rats. "The vast number of rats inhabiting the rocky crevices and cavernous passages at the summit of Pikes Peak, Colorado, have recently become formidable and dangerous," began the story. "Since the establishment of the station, at an altitude of nearly 15,000 feet, these animals have acquired a voracious appetite for raw meat, the scent of which seems to impart to them a ferocity rivaling the starved Siberian wolf."

The story went on to recount that several days earlier, upon O'Keefe's return to the signal station from Colorado Springs, he was startled by his wife's screaming. A horde of enormous rats was pouring out of the O'Keefe bedroom.

Mrs. O'Keefe, although "terribly lacerated" from rat bites, cleverly grabbed a length of wire, hooked it up to a battery, and hurled it across the room, electrocuting many of the vicious rodents. Sadly, though, the rats had already devoured the couple's infant, leaving "nothing but the peeled and mumbled skull."

The story was picked up by the Denver newspapers, then sent abroad over the wire. Before it had run its course, it was printed in papers in the British Isles, France, Russia, Turkey, and Egypt.

Sympathetic visitors to the top brought flowers to the tiny headstone that O'Keefe had erected there. The well-meaning mourners apparently were not aware that the signal serviceman was a confirmed bachelor. After Price died in 1881, O'Keefe's exploits faded into the past. He retired from the U.S. Signal Service in 1883. The signal station itself, having served its original purpose, was dismantled early in the twentieth century.

PHOTO COURTESY COLORADO HISTORICAL SOCIETY

Myers Avenue or Julian Street

By 1914 Cripple Creek was floundering, enduring the hardships that invariably overtake boomtowns when the ore plays out. So when residents heard that a famous writer from *Collier's Weekly* was working on an article about Cripple Creek, they were elated, hoping it would stimulate tourism.

After hearing fascinating stories of Cripple Creek while hobnobbing with financier Spencer Penrose, Julian Street, a well-known *Collier's* reporter, could not resist visiting the famous gold rush town. Reportedly hung over when his train arrived in Cripple Creek, Street had allowed only 45 minutes to take in the sights. He hurriedly strode to the red-light district of Myers Avenue, engaged a local prostitute in a lengthy conversation, visited her room, and hurried back to the station for the trip east.

When his article "Colorado Springs and Cripple Creek" appeared, it was a lurid description of Cripple Creek's Myers Avenue and its bawdy houses with a few excerpts from his talk with the prostitute, whom he characterized as smelling of "strong, brutal perfume."

The residents of Cripple Creek were outraged. Hundreds of letters and wires were sent to the editors of *Collier's*, protesting the article's accuracy and demanding a refutation. The editors agreed to publish one, providing it met their editorial standards. A piece submitted by a local physician apparently did not meet the criteria, however, and was rejected.

The irate citizens of Cripple Creek held an emergency meeting. Among suggestions for recourse included a governor's proclamation, U.S. Senate action, and lawsuits against Street and *Collier's*. They eventually settled the matter on a lighter note. In a unanimous vote that evening, the city council approved changing the name of Myers Avenue to—what else?—Julian Street.

1917, plunked down $3 million, and hired the architects who had designed Grand Central Station to build his 350-room dream. A year later, bolstered by polo grounds, swimming pools, golf courses, stables, and tennis courts, the Broadmoor was on its way to becoming one of the most talked-about resorts in the nation.

Tourist attractions, health spas, and the prospect of leisurely retirement continued to lure people to Colorado Springs throughout the next several decades. Following the outbreak of World War II, the military influence came into its own. In 1942 Camp Carson (today Fort Carson) was created. Later that year Peterson Air Field sprang up on the eastern plains, followed by the North American Air Defense Command (NORAD) at Ent Air Force Base 15 years later.

In 1966 NORAD moved from Ent and disappeared under the shield of Cheyenne Mountain. Its 25-ton doors now protect the 15 steel buildings erected in the subterranean chambers. The huge mass of computers and communication equipment at NORAD, abuzz 24 hours a day, keeps a vigilant watch on the world's busy skies by tracking and identifying virtually all man-made space objects orbiting the earth.

In June 1955 construction of the U.S. Air Force Academy was begun on 17,000 acres north of the city. Considering that it is now the largest tourist attraction in the area, its acquisition is considered by many to be equal to Bob Womack's good fortune in 1890.

Today Colorado Springs continues to enjoy economic prosperity. Scores of tourist attractions such as Seven Falls, Cave of the Winds, Cheyenne Mountain Zoo, and the North Pole fill the city. Colorado Springs has also become one of the fastest growing high-tech centers in the country (partly because of the military build-up there), and it remains a cultural haven, hosting the Fine Arts Center, the Hall of Presidents, the Pioneer's Museum, the Pro Rodeo Hall of Champions, and the National Carvers Museum, a wood-carving showcase.

The sporting life, which began with cricket and polo, has mushroomed, thrust into the limelight by the 34-acre U.S. Olympic Complex. Under development by the U.S. Olympic Committee since 1977 to

Although the heyday of the Cripple Creek mining district is long past, advanced metallurgy techniques have allowed several mines to reopen in recent years. Here, a worker melts gold ore in a Cripple Creek mine. STEWART M. GREEN

Burros, a necessity in Victor less than a century ago, marvel at the advancements of the automobile age. WENDY SHATTIL

Victor, Colorado, was once known as "the City of Gold." JOHN TELFORD

Top: This assay office in Vistor is a ghost of the past, recalling a golden heritage. JOHN TELFORD

Left: A century ago it cost a nickel a head to herd cattle along the toll-operated Shelf Road. Today passage is free. The destination of the road was and still is Cripple Creek. JOHN TELFORD

The first health club in Victor

The recent popularity of health clubs symbolizes the fitness mania that has swept the nation, encompassing everything from Nautilus machines and juice bars to Jane Fonda workout videos. To the historic town of Victor, however, health clubs are old hat.

In 1895 Warren Woods and his sons Frank and Harry, who together founded Victor, began digging the foundation for the Victor Hotel, a plush lodging the wealthy trio envisioned for their community. After uncovering a surface pocket of ore during the initial excavation, however, the men had a quick change of heart. Instead, the Victor Hotel was built elsewhere, and up went the Gold Coin Mine, a million-dollar bonanza smack in the middle of Victor.

The Woods family was regarded as a generous employer by many people in Victor, who were retained in a variety of mining and construction capacities. The men of the Woods empire demonstrated their good will in grand fashion three years later by constructing a lavish health spa called the Gold Coin Club for the leisurely recreation of their employees.

Modeled after the famous New York Athletic Club, the block-long facility housed a gymnasium, a bowling alley, a pool and game room, a ballroom, a dining hall, and a library. The $40,000 spent on the endeavor by the Woods family was apparently no object.

The club had been open only a few months when the catastrophic Victor Fire leveled it. Undaunted, its owners quickly rebuilt and reopened it to the fanfare of the Gold Coin Club's resident 25-piece band. It fast became one of the most-talked-about haunts in the city.

A Victor showcase for many years, the Gold Coin Club was eventually transformed into a hospital following the decline of the gold mines. Still later it became a private residence. Today it stands empty, testimony to a time before body building and aerobics when employees were already devoting their lunch hours to fitness.

Club in Victor. PHOTO COURTESY DENVER PUBLIC LIBRARY, WESTERN HISTORY DEPARTMENT

sponsor the annual National Sports Festival for young athletes, the 59,000-square-foot Sports Center boasts six gymnasiums

The military influence, which is now responsible for 50 percent of the economy and one out of three jobs, has the tightest hold. Colorado Springs has recently become headquarters for the U.S. Air Force Space Command, charged with developing space-oriented defense activities.

Zebulon Pike would have been astounded. Less than two centuries after his wanderings in Pikes Peak Country, which he admitted were "far from the scrutinized eye of civilized man," skyscrapers, space centers, and superhighways have replaced the wilderness he so agonizingly charted.

Broadmoor Lake is the still point around which the Broadmoor complex, above, with its stylish restaurants and three luxurious hotels, revolves. Its founder, Colorado Springs tycoon Spencer Penrose, also financed the Pikes Peak and Cheyenne Mountain highways. STEWART M. GREEN

Guests enjoy feeding the ducks on a leisurely paddleboat cruise around the lake, right. MICHAEL S. SAMPLE

Stairway to heaven

Hewn atop an 800-foot-high hogback in 1906 by prison convicts wielding blasting powder, shovels, and picks, Skyline Drive towers over Canon City as a dazzling piece of roadsmanship.

So narrow is the one-way thoroughfare that it seems the sensitive traveler might topple off either side with the slightest attack of vertigo. And in salute to the great dinosaur graveyards in the region, it is as much a drive up the back of a gigantic stegosaurus as it is a county road cut on top of the sandy Dakota formation.

"Travelers along the Skyline Drive are seen miles away, boldly silhouetted against the sky," reported *Travel Magazine* in 1908. "The town lies clear below you, and you look down on it as if looking at a checkerboard or map, and almost as if poised above it as in a balloon."

The original plans for the road, conceived by Captain Frederick E. Greydene-Smith of Canon City in 1905, called for a scenic drive over a series of hogbacks, the gaps to be spanned by bridges. This idea was abandoned, but it led to the beginning of Skyline Drive construction a year later, initiated with cash donations from local businesses and the cooperation of Colorado State Penitentiary Warden John Cleghorn, whose convicts completed the work in 1907 with hand tools at a total cost of $600.

Originally, only horses and horse-drawn vehicles were permitted to ascend the unique road, which was then entered from the east end of the hogback. With the advent of the automobile age, traveling hours were split equally between horses and internal combustion engines. Today, traffic enters from the west end through a stone-arch gateway. Constructed during the Great Depression by the Work Projects Administration (WPA), this arch contains samples of characteristic minerals from all 48 states at the time, each labeled with the rock's identity and its place of origin.

The panoramic view from the top has remained unchanged. The Sangre de Cristos fill the southern horizon; to the northeast a miniaturized Canon City sprawls like the trimmings of a toy train set. Underneath, literally in the shadow of Skyline Drive, lies the Colorado State Penitentiary, whose earlier inmates toiled to make the road a reality.

Skyline Drive. STEWART M. GREEN

Billed as "the most attractive place of residence in the Rocky Mountains" by founder William Jackson Palmer a century ago, the sheer elegance of the Colorado Springs skyline, above top, is evident today. STEWART M. GREEN

Boots, like these displayed at the Pro Rodeo Hall of Champions and the Museum of the American Cowboy in Colorado Springs, left, are an essential part of the cowboy's wardrobe. KEN GALLARD

The U.S. Olympic Training Center, bottom right, part of the U.S. Olympic Complex in Colorado Springs, offers a residential setting in which athletes can train intensively. KEN GALLARD

As the nation's major supplier of giraffes to zoological parks, the Cheyenne Mountain Zoo, top, is constantly filling tall orders. MICHAEL S. SAMPLE

Parks and picnic areas dot the Pikes Peak region, including this lake, bottom, in Monument Valley. STEWART M. GREEN

Sporting 17 gleaming turrets, Cadet Chapel, above, at the U.S. Air Force Academy is said to be the most photographed subject in Colorado. STEWART M. GREEN

Prior to his founding of Colorado Springs, William J. Palmer was Brigadier General in the Union Army. As the commander of the 15th Pennsylvania Volunteer Cavalry during the Civil War, Palmer directed the pursuit of Confederate troops from Maryland to Georgia. Today, his legacy is commemorated with a statue in downtown Colorado Springs, left. STEWART M. GREEN

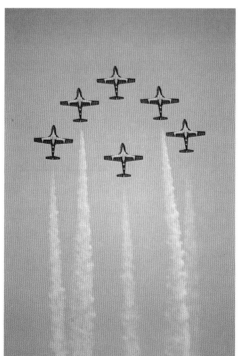

Sunlight filtering through ornate stained glass windows illuminates the interior of Cadet Chapel, above. Completed in 1961, Cadet Chapel is Colorado's most visited tourist attraction of the man-made variety, hosting more than one million people annually.
KEN GALLARD

Jets in formation, left, Colorado Springs. Hosting the U.S. Air Force Academy, Peterson Air Firce Base, the U.S. Air Force Space Command Center, and Fort Carson Army Base, the city is one of the West's major military beehives. STEWART M. GREEN

Solitary horseback rider, above, under the face of Pikes Peak. STEWART M. GREEN

Yellow cinquefoil splashes color below Cathedral Spires on Gold Camp Road, right. STEWART M. GREEN

Leaves of a yucca, opposite page, member of the lily family, whorling outward. Because these plants contain saponin—which produces suds when bruised in water—Indians frequently used yucca as a cleansing agent. PAT O'HARA

Creatures great and small

With more than two vertical miles separating the highest and lowest points in the state, Colorado holds a broad spectrum of wildlife habitat.

Nearly a thousand species of mammals, birds, reptiles, amphibians, and fishes make their living in Colorado. As for plant life, the Front Range alone supports more than 1,500 species of ferns, conifers, and flowering plants as well as hundreds of different mosses, lichens, and liverworts.

Pikes Peak Country itself is a geographical microcosm of the state, rising in altitude from 5,000 feet near Colorado Springs to the 14,110-foot summit of Pikes Peak. The area contains all five ecological life zones represented in Colorado—plains, foothills, montane, subalpine, and alpine.

Much of the flora and fauna of the region is found in the Pike National Forest, more than one million acres of wildlife habitat that was founded in 1907, two years after the creation of the U.S. Forest Service. This national forest is, in addition to a wildlife haven, one of the most popular recreation areas in the state.

For wildlife the dynamics of the area have changed considerably since the early nineteenth century when the first explorers arrived. The Pike expedition, for example, reported capturing two Carolina parakeets (which are now extinct) on the western edge of present-day Fremont County. Stephen Long's 1819 expedition encountered grizzly bears at the base of Pikes Peak.

Edwin James, who chronicled Long's adventure, also reported seeing scores of bison moving up Ute Pass, apparently en route to their grazing grounds in South Park. The last four wild bison in Colorado were killed in 1897 in Lost Park, an isolated valley running out of the northeast corner of South Park.

In this century the major ecological changes have occurred on the rolling plains east of Pikes Peak. Except for isolated pockets, the native shortgrass prairie has been gone for decades. Gray wolves and black-footed ferrets are gone, unable to cope with farms, ranches, highways, and urban development. Fortunately, most wildlife species on the plains are adapting to the presence of more people.

Perhaps none has adjusted as well as the coyote. Its opportunistic habits carry it from high plains habitats into the tundra. Along with the pronghorn, the coyote is perhaps the most representative wildlife species common to the eastern prairie.

Recognizable by its yellowish bars, the tiger salamander is found in glacial kettle ponds, beaver ponds, and plains lakes throughout Pikes Peak Country.
WENDY SHATTIL

The most conspicuous grassland inhabitant may well be the black-tailed prairie dog, whose condominium-like quarters delight many wildlife enthusiasts. Ironically, another resident of these prairie dog colonies has wings. The burrowing owl often shares these tunnels with the rodents, venturing out to hunt in the early mornings and evenings.

The air space over prairie dog towns is often extremely busy. Raptors such as the golden eagle, Swainson's hawk, and prairie falcon soar over the landscape, searching for small rodents and reptiles such as bullsnakes, racers, and earless lizards that have also weathered the civilizing of the Great Plains. Closer to earth, meadowlarks and lark buntings flutter and sing.

Lowland riparian areas like the plains waterways of the Arkansas River and Fountain Creek are the richest ecosystems in the state. This habitat makes up only about 0.2 percent of the total land area in Colorado, but more than 43 percent of all the wildlife species in the state, including 50 percent of the birds, have been recorded there.

Among the most common inhabitants of riparian zones are the American dipper and the beaver. Both can be found along Colorado streams from the prairie to timberline. Flying in beelines up and down Colorado's waterways, dippers are water birds recognizable by their curious bobbing posture. Beavers, after being trapped to the brink of extinction in the early part of the nineteenth century, have made a remarkable comeback.

A myriad of wildlife species live in each life zone, and few are restricted to a specific ecosystem. Many species inhabit more than one life zone, depending on the availability of food, cover, and water.

For a journey through the life zones of the Pikes Peak region, few tours are as well laid out ecologically and perhaps none as scenically as the drive up Phantom Canyon to Victor. Between Canon City and Penrose, where Eightmile Creek flows from the north into the Arkansas River, Colorado State Highway 67 leads the way.

Approximately three miles north into Phantom Canyon from its departure from U.S. Highway 50, the foothills life zone comes into view. Characterized by the food-rich pinyon pine-juniper forests, this zone supports a variety of seasonal wildlife residents. Mule deer and elk winter here, and predators such as bobcats, mountain lions, and weasels often den

nearby, making their living on various species of rabbits and rodents. Pinyon jays, the most familiar bird of this ecosystem, congregate here year-round in raucous flocks. In addition, such avian species as the downy woodpecker, common nighthawk, brown towhee, and black-billed magpie flit in and out of the pinyon-juniper forests during their seasonal movements.

In more arid areas, eastern fence lizards and western rattlesnakes share the rocky floor. In the wetter riparian zones of the pinyon-juniper environment, two of the most common reptiles and amphibians are the western terrestrial garter snake and the northern leopard frog.

At Brush Hollow Reservoir, three miles east of Phantom Canyon (a popular place for such frogs and snakes), live several of the most common warm water fish species found in the Pikes Peak area. Located just north of Penrose, this impoundment hosts largemouth bass, black crappie, bluegill, and channel catfish.

Five miles farther up the canyon, ponderosa pine forests mixed with red cedar and pinyon appear on the south side of the road. Bird life is thick in Colorado's ponderosa stands, which generally grow in sunny, dry areas. In the summer, warblers, hummingbirds, and vireos join ravens, nuthatches, and Stellar's jays. During the spring and summer months, great horned owls and redtailed hawks prowl the forest on silent wings.

A variety of small mammals such as the Colorado chipmunk, golden-mantled ground squirrel, and deer mouse inhabit the ponderosa pine forests. Perhaps the most eye-catching mammal is the Abert's squirrel, recognizable by its enormous ears. Relying almost exclusively on the ponderosa, this squirrel lives on pine cones in the summer and on the inner bark of ponderosa twigs during winter.

Beyond the second railroad tunnel—blasted out a century ago—Douglas firs begin to take over portions of the forest. These Douglas fir stands, mixing easily with the pine, host many of the same wildlife species. A bit higher in elevation, they also support pine squirrels, ruby-crowned kinglets, and hermit thrushes.

Soon the canyon breaks into aspen groves, a major tourist attraction of Pikes Peak Country each autumn. These deciduous forests are successional, appearing at elevations of 8,000 to 10,000 feet when conifers

Historic transplants of elk into the Pikes Peak region, including 55 shipped by rail from Yellowstone National Park to Pikes Peak by local financier Spencer Penrose in 1915, may be in part responsible for the increase in these animals during the past century. Wildlife biologists believe that elk suffered a statewide decline late last century due to commercial hunting and habitat alteration. MICHAEL S. SAMPLE

An unparalleled engineer in the animal world, the beaver is adapted to an aquatic life. Its valve-like ears and nose close off, clear membranes slide over its eyes, and flaps of skin seal its mouth as the beaver submerges underwater. WENDY SHATTIL

For hikers who have heard its shrill signal for more than a mile away, the marmot's nickname of "whistle-pig" is appropriate. Marmots tend to be on the obese side, packing up to nine pounds on their 26-inch-long frame. WENDY SHATTIL

The return of the peregrine falcon

The endangered peregrine falcon, virtually erased from the continental United States, is slowly returning to Pikes Peak Country.

These raptors historically occurred throughout Colorado, although they were never common. In the Pikes Peak region, they were reported in the vicinity of the U.S. Air Force Academy, Garden of the Gods, and Royal Gorge.

Unfortunately, the indiscriminate use of DDT ravaged populations nationwide beginning in the 1950s. This pesticide inhibited the metabolism of calcium in a variety of breeding raptors, including peregrines. If the paper-thin eggshells were not broken during the laying process, possibilities were high that they would be shattered during incubation.

DDT was banned for use in the United States in 1971, but that was almost too late. A year later there were no successful pairs of peregrines nesting anywhere in the state. In 1976 the Colorado Division of Wildlife, in cooperation with the National Park Service, the U.S. Forest Service, the Bureau of Land Management, and the Peregrine Fund, began an intensive reintroduction program, funded in part by Colorado's nongame income tax check-off program.

Since then more than 460 peregrines have been released into Colorado's wilds. In some cases, eggs have been taken from wild pairs, hatched in laboratories, and returned to their nests. In addition, scores of peregrine chicks have been hatched at the Peregrine Fund's raptor facility in Boise, Idaho, then raised in "hack boxes" atop historical eyries and fed until they were able to fend for themselves.

One of the most successful hacking boxes in Colorado was located to the west of Cheyenne Mountain. Since 1983 a total of 16 birds were fledged there. "One of the most remarkable things about this site," said Jerry Craig, the Division's raptor biologist who is coordinating the statewide reintroduction effort, "is that we had 100 percent success there."

Another hack site in the Royal Gorge was abandoned by biologists in 1985 following severe predation on the peregrine chicks by great horned owls. The operation has since been moved to a site south of Cripple Creek.

In 1993, 53 pairs of peregrines were breeding in Colorado, including one that has reoccupied an historical eyrie west of Cheyenne Mountain. Craig, who has dedicated much of the last two decades to raptor work, is philosophical about his efforts. "It was a long, slow, discouraging, and expensive process," he admitted. "But we owe it to these birds, and I think we can finally see the light at the end of the tunnel."

"Stooping" at nearly 200 miles per hour in pursuit of prey, the dive of the peregrine falcon has been described as sounding like the rush of a blowtorch.
W. PERRY CONWAY

The horns and skull of a Rocky Mountain bighorn ram, which may weigh up to 50 pounds, are tremendous weapons when used against each other during the mating season. The rams—which may reach a height of 40 inches at the shoulder and weigh 300 pounds—are polygamous, with up to 10 ewes in each ram's harem.
MICHAEL S. SAMPLE

have been removed by fire, logging, or disease.

Smaller carnivores such as the montane shrew and long-tailed weasel are common in these aspen groves, which are often mixed with lodgepole pine. Silver-haired bats are also common, and elk use these areas for calving grounds.

Elk were apparently scarcer in the region during the latter half of the nineteenth century, possibly due to the intense "market hunting" of the animals that occurred in the vicinity of many western settlements. Transplants during this century have bolstered populations, however. The present Pikes Peak elk herd may be descended from the herd brought in from the Yellowstone region by Colorado Springs tycoon Spencer Penrose in 1915 to stock his private game preserve.

The vast acreage of mountain grasslands at the higher elevations of Pikes Peak Country, especially from Victor north through Mueller State Park, the Florissant Valley, and beyond into the Tarryall Range, is a boon to wildlife. Here predator and prey alike dwell on the forest's edge, moving in and out of the meadows, disappearing and reappearing from the thick tree stands.

Rainbow, brown, brook, and cutthroat trout also reside in the higher elevations of the region's aquatic environments. Kokanee salmon, close cousins of the trout, also inhabit some of the reservoirs that dot the South Platte River System, as does the brawling northern pike, which may grow in excess of 20 pounds.

Among wildlife havens, few places are as spectacular as the Mueller State Park. Located 17 miles due west of Pikes Peak, this 12,000-acre

Looking for lions

"The Canon City area has all the characteristics of good lion habitat," said Bob Hernbrode, former big game manager for the Colorado Division of Wildlife. "It's that broken country with a lot of topographical relief and high deer populations that seem to suit these animals the best."

This was one of the reasons that the town of Victor was chosen as headquarters of a mountain lion study in the mid-1970s. A joint effort between Colorado State University (C.S.U.) and the Colorado Division of Wildlife, the project was designed to bring this species to bay in order to ensure its survival.

The study, headed by C.S.U. graduate student Mary Jean Currier, took place over a three-year period from 1974-1977. During the course of the study (which was soon expanded to the northern edge of Custer County and west almost to Salida), 29 mountain lions were tranquilized, captured, and released. In addition, some 262 separate sets of tracks were documented by the researchers.

"I think that most [people] would be very surprised if they knew just what was roaming in the foothills of the Front Range," said Hernbrode. "Almost without exception, when researchers begin looking for lions, they find more than they first anticipated."

Deer are the mainstay of the mountain lion's diet, but they are opportunistic enough to also feed on elk, rabbits, rodents, and even porcupines. Using their speed and great leaping ability (they are able to bound up to 40 feet in one leap), lions run their prey down and quickly dispatch them. Incredibly strong, they have been known to carry deer up steep cliffs and to drag elk for some distance.

Although the record weight for the North American mountain lion is 276 pounds (shot by Teddy Roosevelt in Colorado during the early 1900s), they usually average 100 to 160 pounds, with the significantly larger males reaching eight feet in length. The cubs, born with spots in late winter or early spring, may stay with the mother for up to two years.

Mountain lions are the most widespread mammal in the Western Hemisphere, ranging from the tip of South America to British Columbia, haunting jungle to tundra. In Colorado they can be found most anywhere large populations of deer exist, even far out onto the eastern plains.

As with many other wildlife species, lions are having increasing numbers of conflicts with man. In 1985 an incident at Perry Park, a posh mountain development southwest of Castle Rock, involved several of the big cats prowling through the subdivision and grabbing domestic pets and national headlines. One lion, later killed by federal government trappers, was suspected of having been fed as a cub by a resident there.

The major problem, however, is one of space. Perry Park and other new housing projects have been constructed on some of the best mountain lion habitat in Colorado. As long as the Front Range continues to expand, these human-wildlife conflicts will increase as well.

The Canon City mountain lion study concluded that the population of these big cats was relatively high and did not appear to be in danger of being overhunted. Like many species of wildlife, mountain lions have proven to be fairly flexible in terms of their habitat. Are people flexible enough to accommodate them?

Female mountain lion and yearling romp in a snowfield. Kittens may stay close by the mother until they are one to two years old. W. PERRY CONWAY

parcel of wildland is administered by the Colorado Department of Natural Resources (CDNR). Purchased in 1979 from private landowners by the Nature Conservancy (a private conservation foundation dedicated to the acquisition of ecologically significant lands), the bulk of the acreage was subsequently resold to the CDNR as a park and wildlife refuge.

The Mueller State Park is currently made up of several parcels. The 7,000-acre southern portion, managed as a wildlife area, is an astounding place to observe animals. In addition to a resident herd of bighorn sheep, there are black bears, mountain lions, bobcats, deer, and elk living on the property. The bird life varies enormously, from eagles to wild turkeys to songbirds.

The northern portion, nearly 5,000 acres in all, has been developed for recreational use. A third parcel, the 640-acre Dome Rock Natural Area, contains the spectacular geologic formation of Dome Rock that acts as a landmark for the entire Mueller State Park.

Although the grizzly was hunted to extinction in Colorado, black bears are fairly common. Because these omnivores require many different kinds of foods in their diet (relying mainly on plant species for their energy requirements), they use a wide range of habitat. The Pikes Peak region meets their needs superbly. The distance between the pinyon-juniper forests and the alpine tundra is relatively small, allowing black bears to move thousands of vertical feet in short order.

They move too much for some people's liking. In recent years there have been an inordinate number of bear and human conflicts west of Manitou Springs, usually revolving around the refuse of growing developments.

As the region's dominant mountain above timberline, Pikes Peak is a showcase for elevated environments. The dark green sheen of the Engelmann spruce and subalpine fir forests, skirting the mountain's shoulders at elevations between 9,000 and 12,000 feet, is visible for miles. Here pine martens dwell in the dimness, as do snowshoe hares, which

Duplicating lizards

For the checkered whiptail lizard, an unusual resident of Pikes Peak Country, it is definitely a woman's world.

The reason is simple. Since the rare, abnormal males that occur in the species are sterile and short-lived, the population is essentially all female in gender. By a quirk of genetic fate, they possess the ability to clone themselves, producing mirror images without the benefit of a mating partner. This makes them "like mother, like daughter."

This peculiar form of reproduction is accomplished by parthenogenesis, in which the embryo develops without fertilization. The offspring theoretically contain 100 percent of the mother's biological characteristics, down to the tiniest freckle, although minute genetic variations invariably occur.

This process has its advantages. By bypassing the often cumbersome courtship proceedings, these reptiles can just head over the hill and start a new colony any time they like. On the down side, they are best suited to areas of little climatic change, since any variation in the environment could be devastating to these populations, which have no genetic variability.

The checkered whiptail, which ranges from the foothills between Cripple Creek and Canon City all the way south to Mexico, is a medium-sized lizard about three and a half inches long, sporting a tail nearly twice that length. Inhabiting sparsely vegetated canyons, bluffs, and gullies, these lizards are incredibly swift, running down their prey—flies, grasshoppers, crickets, and ants—with ease.

They are thought by herpetologists to have arisen through hybridization between several other species of whiptails probably only a few centuries ago. Barring any climatic disasters, these lady lizards will likely continue to grace the Pikes Peak region with duplicates of themselves for centuries to come.

With the unusual ability to produce young without the benefit of fertilization, female checkered whiptail lizards essentially clone mirror images of themselves.
STEWART M. GREEN

*Few sounds are more haunting than the bugle of
a bull elk during rutting season.* MICHAEL S. SAMPLE

*Termed "prairie smoke," this long-plumed avens
can be found from medium-dry plains, hillsides,
and ridges to over 8,000 feet in elevation. Indians
boiled the roots to make a drink which tastes
much like weak sassafras tea.* MICHAEL S. SAMPLE.

change their coats to match the seasons. Clark's nutcrackers, gray jays, and mountain chickadees, each with a keen curiosity towards human intruders, make the subalpine life zone their home.

The transition zone from these thick forests to the tundra is an extremely harsh one. Bizarre one-sided trees and stunted shrubs testify to the constant howling winds. The trees here have met their match against the extreme cold, drought, and incessant wind, halting their upward procession. To biologists, the ecosystem is called the "krummholz," meaning "crooked wood" in German.

Above it all, on the highest slopes of Pikes Peak, is the windswept tundra. "The key to understanding the tundra ecosystem is to reduce one's sense of scale," wrote Cornelia Fleischer Mutel and John C. Emerick in their classic study of Colorado's natural history, *From Grassland to Glacier*. "One needs to get down on hands and knees to see the ecosystems, as well as to see the tremendous variation in communities and environments that can occur in one small area."

Spectacular wildflower displays are the trademark of the tundra. The wildlife, including pika, marmot, ptarmigan, and bighorn sheep, is eerily conspicuous, having few places to hide. Two of the most common and curious residents are the pika and the marmot, unlikely bedfellows at first glance.

This is especially evident in their contrasting expenditures of energy. A member of the rabbit family, the pika is a scurrier, frenetically gathering grasses and wildflowers for the haystacks it hides under rocks for use during the winter. The marmot, on the other hand, seems less concerned, alternately sunning itself, whistling, and grazing. These obese "whistle-pigs" seem to know that while their nervous neighbors will spend most of the winter alert, nibbling at their caches through the savage alpine storms, they will be locked in a deep slumber.

Although ptarmigan are now quite common residents of the Pikes Peak tundra, this wasn't always the case. After long wondering why they were absent from the environment there, Division of Wildlife biologists finally decided to introduce several flocks onto the peak beginning in May 1975. Today they are thriving.

The Rocky Mountain bighorn sheep are the most conspicuous residents of the tundra, although they range widely in other life zones. The Pikes Peak herd has always been one of Colorado's most famous wildlife attractions, and the Tarryall herd to the northwest was at one time the largest bighorn sheep herd in the United States, numbering well over a thousand.

Although both herds have suffered periodic population crashes during the past century as victims of lungworm, which appears to be a symptom of stress caused by the fragmentation of their habitat, Rocky Mountain bighorns remain the official seal of Colorado's wildlands. Presiding over Pikes Peak Country, they are living logos of the wilderness. Alone at the top, they symbolize the diversity and endless beauty of the region.

Also known as cranesbill because of its elongated fruit, wild geraniums are not only a delight to humans who wander by but also a valuable forage plant for elk and deer. MICHAEL S. SAMPLE

As one of the noisiest residents of the region, the chickaree's ratchet-like call generally announces its presence high in lodgepole pine and aspen forests. These animals often have a favorite feeding perch, as evidenced by the mounds of pine cone shucks below. In the winter, they often tunnel in the snow. WENDY SHATTIL

When in full bloom during late June, July, and early August, Indian paintbrush, left, can color entire valleys. These plants are parasitic, penetrating the roots of nearby plants with their own in order to steal nutrients. MICHAEL S. SAMPLE

Above right: This mule deer buck finds scanty cover in the forest tundra transition zone known as the Krommholz. WENDY SHATTIL

Colorado's greatest grizzly

The May 3, 1904, headline in the *Denver Post* told the story succinctly: "Old Mose Has Bit The Dust."

Colorado's most notorious grizzly bear, whose quarter-century rampage through Pikes Peak Country won him the reputation of the fiercest man or beast ever to prowl the territory, was dead. His legacy was grim. During his reign, Old Mose was credited with killing three men and scores of sheep and cattle, striking terror and fury into the hearts of residents.

His home, for the most part, was the wooded flanks of Black Mountain and Thirtynine Mile Mountain, about 35 miles northwest of Canon City. His range was said to be a good deal larger, encompassing much of south-central Colorado and as far west as the Utah border.

Because of his infamy, the great bear was pursued relentlessly for more than two decades by professional hunters, irate stockmen, and anyone else with uncommon courage. Following the death of his first human victim, Jake Ratcliffe of Fairplay, whom he fatally mauled in 1882, the chase began in earnest.

Because of his size, estimated to be well over 1,000 pounds, Old Mose easily shrugged off most attempts on his life, including numerous unsuccessful trapping incidents and at least a dozen gunshot wounds. The more the hunters failed, the more the bear grew in stature and reputation; indeed, he became larger than life.

The end for Old Mose came on a springlike morning. James W. Anthony, a professional hunter from Boise, Idaho, who was bunking at Wharton Pigg's Stirrup Ranch just south of Black Mountain, picked up a fresh trail with the aid of dogs only three miles from the ranch. As quickly as it began, it was over.

"The old terror of the cattlemen, ranchers, prospectors, and fishermen met his death in a manner befitting many of his deeds and violence on the range without a flinch and without a groan," according to the *Post's* account, "carrying six bullets which cut him through and through, still coming in a slow deliberate walk toward the man who was hurling the death-dealing missiles from a 30-40 Winchester."

The carcass was brought to Canon City for viewing, then taken west by Anthony. It was subsequently willed to the zoology department of the University of California at Berkeley, where it is today. The memory of Old Mose remains in Pikes Peak Country, however, a keepsake of a woollier time. Old Mose, despite his reputation, was nothing more than a wild creature, peaceable when left alone. Born too late, he battled the changing times with an uncanny instinct and a terrible power. And Old Mose finally lost.

Old Mose met his match in 1904. PHOTO COURTESY OF ROCKY MOUNTAIN NEWS

A year-round resident of the Pikes Peak tundra, the ptarmigan, above, survives by bedding in snow drifts and feeding on energy-rich willow buds. WENDY SHATTIL

Often blooming before the snows have even melted, marshmarigolds, bottom, grow in moist subalpine regions between 7,000 and 10,000 feet. MICHAEL S. SAMPLE.

Mule deer, above, the most common large mammals found in Pikes Peak Country, are always alert.
WENDY SHATTIL

Bird's-nest fungi, left, rise out of bark, twigs, and debris in the ponderosa pine forests of the Pikes Peak region. Often tucked deep in the inaccessible reaches of the forest, these fungi are probably marveled about more often in conversation than actually seen. WENDY SHATTIL

Wildlife

Although the diminutive pika, top left, weighs only about seven ounces, its deep, nasal chirp is audible far down the landscape. Found from 8,500 feet to the tundra, the charismatic pika is a familiar sight—and sound—to hikers and packpackers. WENDY SHATTIL

Much like its relative the snowshoe hare, this cottontail, lower left, is at home in snowy environs. Cottontails feed on almost anything green during the spring and summer months, switching over to bark, twigs, and buds during the harsh winters. WENDY SHATTIL

Also known as tassel-eared squirrels, the Abert's squirrel, bottom right, is a common resident of ponderosa forests. Colorado hosts a high number of melanistic (black) individuals, which posses an increased amount of pigmentation in their fur.
WENDY SHATTIL

A clumsy lumberer at best, the porcupine is much more at home in trees than on terra firma. These animals feed on twigs, and are covered with sharp, spiny quills to repel predators. WENDY SHATTIL

Enjoying Pikes Peak Country

The Front Range of Colorado's Rockies has become a bona fide hub. Today the Eastern Slope harbors about three million people. Since the farthest away of these inhabitants lives only a two-and-a-half-hour's drive from Pikes Peak Country—and the closest smack in its breast—this region is a tailor-made getaway. Whether it be for hiking, camping, picnicking, fishing, whitewater rafting, bicycling, skiing, rock climbing, backpacking, or sight-seeing, few places in the West can compare.

Since the earliest days, the summit of the huge mountain has been the focus of many people's attention. The fascination with the top, beginning with Pike's unsuccessful bid, was followed by commercial burro and carriage ascents during the late 1800s, a cog railway, and an automobile road. A quarter-million people now drive to the top of Pikes Peak annually, while thousands of others hike, run, and even race cars to the clouds.

The first auto arrived in 1901, when W.B. Felkner and C.A. Yont drove (and pushed) their innovative Locomobile to the top. Since 1916, with the exception of the war years, the renowned Pikes Peak Hill Climb has taken place every July. Appropriately billed as one of the most unusual car races in the world, this 12.4-mile course screams through 156 tortuous curves.

In the past, vintage racers like Barney Oldfield participated in the challenge. Lately, such gentlemen as Mario Andretti, Parnelli Jones, and Rick and Roger Mears regularly started their engines there. Perhaps no racing clan has so dominated the Pikes Peak Hill Climb as the Unsers: Al, Bobby, and Al junior have finished in the roses no fewer than 28 times in at least one of the race's three class divisions.

Each August hundreds of runners suck it up and head for the top of Pikes Peak via the Barr Trail in one of the most grueling marathon competitions in the world. Because of its curious layout, a 7,700-foot vertical climb up and down the 14,110-foot peak, this particular endurance contest (the second-oldest marathon in the United States behind the Boston Marathon) attracts a dedicated if slightly masochistic crew.

In 1986 elementary schoolteacher Stanley Fox of

As one of the major amateur sports centers in the nation, Colorado Springs hosted the World Cycling Championships. The 160-mile race was held at the U.S. Air Force Academy.
GARY SPRING/GNURPS

Picnickers enjoy lunch at Palmer Park, over-looking Colorado Springs. STEWART M. GREEN

Gunnison made his seventh bid for the course title. His time of 3:41:57 set the standard on that particular race day. "I'm so happy I could cry," panted an exhausted Fox following the 26.2-mile run, "and I felt I would a couple of times coming down the mountain."

Margie Loyd-Allison of Colorado Springs finished the Pikes Peak Marathon with the winning time of 4:55:43 in the women's division in 1986. She crossed the finish line sporting some ugly scrapes on her hands and legs. "Merely flesh wounds," she shrugged afterwards. "They say you haven't run on the Pikes Peak trail until you've fallen on it."

Every step of the way, both runners and hikers to the top owe their favor to Fred Barr, a prototypical outdoorsman who enjoyed an unusual hobby. From 1916 to 1921 he spent his winters toiling in the mines and saving his money for his summer pastime of purchasing kegs of blasting powder and blowing out the 14-mile trail to the top of Pikes Peak. Today the journey along Barr Trail is enjoyed

and endured by thousands annually, making Pikes Peak the most scaled Fourteener in the state.

This propensity for ascension in Pikes Peak Country is not limited to the mountain. Technical rock climbing on the region's wealth of spires, domes, and pinnacles has become an addiction of sorts to many. Perhaps the most striking location for those inclined to clamber is the Garden of the Gods, where the bizarre sandstone formations test the mettle of even the most experienced mountaineers.

One of the main reasons for the Garden's popularity is its accessibility. Other climbing hotspots in the Pikes Peak region (including Sheep's Nose and Turkey Rock north of Woodland Park, Elevenmile Canyon, and the Crags behind Pikes Peak) are quite popular, but they mean using up valuable climbing time behind the wheel.

In contrast, local climbers who frequent the Garden can be at their destination and uncoiling their ropes in minutes.

The same erosive forces that shaped the spires and towers millions of years ago make climbing there today an ever-changing test of will and skill. Even a cloudburst can add new dimensions to some of the routes. "The really heavy rains can make things extremely sandy again,"explains Lou Kalina, a Garden aficionado who works in a local mountaineering shop. "Some of the regular climbers even carry along paint brushes to dust off the holds."

Dan Heidenreich, a geologist by training and a climber by passion, pointed out that *Soft Touch,* a climbing guidebook that highlights the hundreds of routes over the Garden's sandstone, is appropriately named. "When you climb there every day, the rock begins to feel real solid to you," he says. "You know that some of the flakes are loose, and that the rocks can break, but by and large, you get a good feel for it.

"But when you go off and climb on harder rock for a while, and then jump back to climbing in the Garden again, it can be a rude awakening," he says. "It can be extremely rude for visiting climbers from other parts of the country that aren't used to the softer rock."

For residents and visitors who practice less strenuous hobbies, fishing in the Pikes Peak region is perhaps the most time-honored outdoor tradition. The key is the South Platte River, the most famous

An annual balloon rally is part of the Labor Day festivities in Colorado Springs' Memorial Park.
STEWART M. GREEN

The brainchild of Colorado Springs financier Spencer Penrose, the 18.8-mile Pikes Peak Highway was opened for business in 1916 at a cost of $500,000. Originally operated as a toll road, the highway became a free road in 1936, reverting to its toll status in the 1940s because of the high maintenance costs. Rising some 6,719 feet from Cascade to its termination at the Summit House, the highway is the second-highest automobile road in the U.S.—only slightly lower than the road up Mount Evans near Denver.

Pikes Peak toll road. PHOTO COURTESY OF COLORADO HISTORICAL SOCIETY

First autos on the Pikes Peak toll road. PHOTO COURTESY OF COLORADO HISTORICAL SOCIETY

angling waters in the state. The waterway, which now ties together a massive reservoir system, has had to trade some of its choicest riffles for impoundments. While this swap of one angling resource for another has diminished the wildness of the region, it has nevertheless been intriguing in terms of fisheries management.

Because of its proximity to Colorado Springs and Denver, the entire chain of reservoirs along the South Platte River system receives intense fishing pressure. In addition to the Spinney Mountain bonanza, the Elevenmile, Antero, and Tarryall reservoirs are all extremely popular with anglers, boaters, campers, and picnickers. No stretch of water in the state is more famous for its excellent trout fishing, however, than the section of the Platte directly below Cheesman Canyon.

The Arkansas River, a popular fishing haven in its own right, is renowned more for its roaring white water than its trout. Some 100,000 people take to the river annually in rafts and kayaks, making it the favored Front Range waterway for Colorado's 250,000 river rats.

One of the most popular stretches is the run from Texas Creek to a point just above the Royal Gorge, paralleled by U.S. Highway 50. The section of water just below that flows through the Gorge is by all accounts the most dangerous part of the river. It was not until the 1950s that anyone attempted to run the rapids there, and even now overturned boats through that section seem to be as much the rule as the exception. As many as 50 rafting outfitters operate along the waterway during a typical summer season, so the thrill is definitely the careening froth, not the solitude.

For those in search of serenity, there is the Lost Creek Wilderness Area, located in the Tarryall Mountains to the northwest of Colorado Springs. Once inside its bounds, hikers can forget the frantic pace of the Front Range cities lying only an hour's drive away.

This abrupt shift from highways, hotels, and horns to a roadless wilderness is one of deafening silence.

The wilderness area is a relatively small portion of the enormous Pike National Forest, whose 1,105,000 acres engulf the bulk of Pikes Peak Country. The wilderness gets its name from Lost Creek, one of the odder waterways in the state. On at least nine separate occasions through the wilder-

As the nation's unofficial mountain running championship, the Pikes Peak Marathon has some serious ups and downs. The 26.2-mile course climbs 7,700 vertical feet before turning at the summit for the prolonged descent. STEWART M. GREEN

ness, it disappears underground in a series of "sinks," only to reappear farther downstream. During its final underground odyssey, the stream changes names, resurfacing several hundred yards downstream as Goose Creek, about six miles from the popular Goose Creek trailhead.

These bizarre sinks, which vary in underground length from a few hundred feet to more than half a mile, are intriguing, to say the least. They are made more so by the unsubstantiated reports of people attempting to swim through the subterranean channels.

Four miles up the Goose Creek trail, a collection of dilapidated ranch buildings stands off to the left in a meadow. Alongside one of the buildings, a rectangular outline of white quartz chunks marks the grave of a prospector named Palmer, who died in 1930.

A side trail west from the cabins leads to the Shafthouse a mile beyond. The caved-in excavation, littered with a rusting steam hoist and an upended boiler, testifies to the Denver Water Board's $325,000 attempt to dam the underground stream of Goose Creek and to build a reservoir there during the early part of the century.

Naming the hundreds of magnificent granite outcroppings is one of the favorite games of hikers. These rock formations, more than anything else, are the signature of the Lost Creek Wilderness. Domes, halfdomes, minarets, and spires are visible from virtually all of its dozens of miles of trails. So is 12,431-foot Bison Peak, which bounds the wilderness area on the southwest.

One of the criteria for defining a true wilderness area, according to federal land management agencies, is that it afford a genuine opportunity for solitude. The Beaver Creek Wilderness Study Area has no trouble meeting this criterion, despite its location on the Front Range. Covering more than 26,000 acres between Canon City and the southern slopes of Pikes Peak, this wilderness area, from the semi-arid shrubland in the south, host to candelabra cactus and western rattlesnakes, to the 10,000-foot granite knobs that loom above fir, aspen, bighorns, and black bears, is a study in diversity.

Beaver Creek itself forms a lush riparian ecosystem that threads through 11 miles of twisting canyon. The main fork of Beaver Creek, only a few feet wide in places during the late summer, rampages freely in the spring, evidenced by the logjams of cottonwood and ponderosa strewn about the bottom land.

The fish that reside there are an absolute delight. At the lower end patient brown trout fin in the shadows of the cottonwoods that line the banks. Up top, some 3,000 feet higher in elevation, native cutthroat rest in the riffles, shadowed by spruce trees. In between, both brookies and rainbows cruise the clear, cool water of this drainage, making it one of the few waterways in the state offering anglers a legitimate shot at the "Grand Slam" of all four trout species from a single creek.

The trail is a ghost of a path high up on the east side of the creek, shining with mica at every step. In places it also gleams with flakes of flint discarded centuries ago by tool-making Indians and washed down the gullies from their ancient campsites.

In the shrubland, canyon wrens trill their descending scale, a contrast to the alpine chirps of pika and marmot that most Colorado wilderness enthusiasts are accustomed to. From deep in the gloom of a pinyon, juniper, and oakbrush stand, wild turkeys appear briefly, only to be swallowed up by the shadows.

During the past two centuries, the Pikes Peak region has undergone dramatic changes. Skyscrapers, subdivisions, superhighways, and military installations have moved into the once wild plains and foothills; towns, resorts, and mines have encroached on the mountain wilderness.

Still, a wealth of pristine places remains. Some of the most spectacular areas in the region, including the Lost Creek Wilderness Area, the Florissant Fossil Beds, and Mueller State Park, have been preserved in all their wild glory for future generations. Others, like the Beaver Creek Wilderness Study Area, are in limbo.

From its earliest days, the overwhelming beauty of Pikes Peak has been intimately tied to its fortunes. Whether the reasons for its initial preservation were economic, altruistic, or the more likely combination of both doesn't really matter; the bottom line is that many of these places remain in a natural state for all to admire. The Royal Gorge will probably never be dammed, and the only thief looting the Garden of the Gods is erosion.

But because of its grandeur, the region is threatened by an ironic shadow. Pikes Peak Country has the very real potential of being loved to death in its natural state by the millions of visitors and new residents that will come to marvel at its wonders during the next century.

Pikes Peak Country undoubtedly holds a special place in the hearts of many today. A ride over Gold Camp Road in late September, the fiery aspens lighting the way to Cripple Creek at high noon, is enough to carry even the most tropical-minded of us through another winter and into spring again. This capacity of Pikes Peak Country to transcend both seasons and miles will always bring us back.

A young fisherman awaits his catch along the edge of Manitou Lake, Pike National Forest, left. STEWART M. GREEN

Anglers, below, hoist their catch— three native cutthroat and one brown trout—at Spinney Mountain Reservoir in South Park, one of the better angling properties in Colorado.
GARY SPRUNG/GNURPS

79

Left: A climber scales "Quiver and Quill" on Turkey's Tail north of Colorado Springs. STEWART M. GREEN

Below right: A solo climber spans a chimney on Turkey Rock. STEWART M. GREEN

Ute Pass boulders, bottom left, are the perfect place for climbers to hone their climbing skills. STEWART M. GREEN

Anglers in Elevenmile Canyon, top, fishing from the same bank that Zebulon Pike traversed in his search for the Red River nearly two centuries ago. JOE ARNODL JR.

For farmers, fishermen, businessmen, and leisure-time aficionados, water is the key in Pikes Peak Country, bottom left.
MICHAEL S. SAMPLE

Even in an arid state like Colorado, two small girls, bottom right, enjoy tubing in Pikes Peak Country. MICHAEL S. SAMPLE

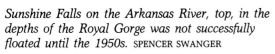

Sunshine Falls on the Arkansas River, top, in the depths of the Royal Gorge was not successfully floated until the 1950s. SPENCER SWANGER

A kayaker, left, takes Sunshine Falls. SPENCER SWANGER

Sunshine Falls on the Arkansas River, bottom right, provides thrills for some adventuresome river rafters. SPENCER SWANGER

An angler's dream

Ever since the first "Fish Train" began running anglers out of Denver to the waters of the South Platte River a hundred years ago, Cheesman Canyon has been the stuff of fishing legends.

Located just south of Deckers, Cheesman Canyon is within an hour's drive of nearly two million people. Despite its accessibility, this stretch of the South Platte is considered by fisheries biologists and sportsmen alike to be the finest stream fishing in the lower 48 states located near a major metropolitan area.

According to a sampling undertaken by the Colorado Division of Wildlife, the portion of the river running through Cheesman Canyon has the highest standing stock of trout of any water in the state. Boasting an incredible 400 to 700 pounds of trout per acre, the productivity of Cheesman Canyon is rivaled in Colorado only by the legendary Frying Pan River near Basalt.

Because of its prodigious natural production, a 19.5-mile stretch of the South Platte has been designated as "Gold Medal" trout-fishing water by the Division of Wildlife. This designation represents the highest-quality aquatic habitat that exists in Colorado, providing the best chance to catch large

The fishing is hottest in the first three miles of the canyon downstream from Cheesman Lake, where the deep, clear pools riddled with granite blocks act as enormous holding tanks for the rainbow and brown trout. This three-mile stretch is also a catch-and-release, flies-and-lures-only section, which proves that high catch rates and heavy fishing pressure can coexist.

While a plan to inundate some 30 miles of the South Platte River, including this spectacular gorge, with the proposed Two Forks Dam was beaten back by Colorado's citizens and environmental groups several years ago, nothing is forever.

So take Isaak Walton's time-tested advice and go "A-angling" there. Just to be on the safe side, though, go soon.

Fishing below Cheesman Lake. STEWART M. GREEN

A patch of Gambel oak, top, photographed in the Garden of the Gods. Usually mixed with mountain mahogany, the dark green leaves of the oak, which are often accompanied by petite acorns, turn a brilliant red in the fall. STEWART M. GREEN

Tarryall Creek, right, meanders in a wide bow below the roadless terrain of the Lost Creek Wilderness Area. STEWART M. GREEN

Goose Creek in the Lost Creek Wilderness Area, top. Nearly 100 miles of foot and horse trails crisscross the roadless area. JACK OLSON

Whitetail fawn, bottom left, stands wobbling on unsure feet. These innocent babes are protected not only by their spots but also by being born scentless to help them remain undiscovered by predators during the first few days of their life. MICHAEL S. SAMPLE

A brushy trail winds through the Bear Creek Nature Center, bottom right. More than 150 species of birds have been recorded at this refuge. MICHAEL S. SAMPLE

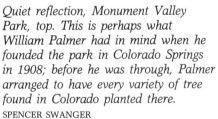

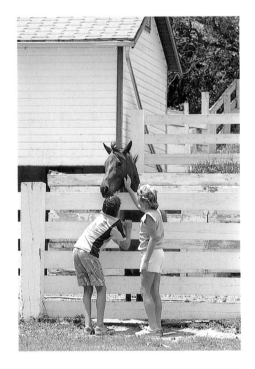

Quiet reflection, Monument Valley Park, top. This is perhaps what William Palmer had in mind when he founded the park in Colorado Springs in 1908; before he was through, Palmer arranged to have every variety of tree found in Colorado planted there.
SPENCER SWANGER

Located adjacent to the Garden of the Gods, the White House Ranch, bottom left, offers visitors the opportunity to relive the history of the Pikes Peak region. The ranch was originally constructed by Scottish homesteader Walter Galloway, who built a log cabin there in 1867 near the banks of Camp Creek. MICHAEL S. SAMPLE

The unusual ranch, bottom right, now a Colorado Springs city park, takes visitors for a stroll back in time by offering a working blacksmith shop from a century ago, a general store, and a number of historical exhibits. STEWART M. GREEN

Memorial Park Labor Day
Festival, Colorado Springs,
above. The sky is the limit
during this annual three-day
festival, which features
skydiving and ultralight
airplane exhibitions in
additions to these hot-air
balloons over Prospect Lake.
SPENCER SWANGER

An ultralight aircraft, right,
touches down in a field below
Pikes Peak. STEWART M. GREEN

Out of the chutes and headlong into the arena, top left, this competitor vies for a title in the bull-riding competition of the Pikes Peak or Bust Rodeo. KEN GALLARD

At top right, a perfect loop flies true during the calf-roping competition. STEWART M. GREEN

A formidable selection of rodeo bucking bulls, bottom left, intimidate prospective riders at the annual Colorado Springs Pikes Peak or Bust Rodeo. KEN GALLARD

Long, cold shadows of quaking aspens, bared by winter's chill, top. Common throughout the region, aspens sprout freely from their snaking, underground tubers, springing up quickly in areas of soil disturbance and providing prime wildlife habitat. STEWART M. GREEN

An early season thunderhead, above right, preparing to discharge yet more snow into the already inundated Pikes Peak region. The "rain shadow" effect of Colorado's Rockies causes moisture-laden clouds bearing east from the Pacific Coast to rise over the mountains and then cool, unloading enormous amounts of precipitation on the peaks. MICHAEL S. SAMPLE

Cross-country skiing, bottom left, in the shadow of the Crags on the west side of Pikes Peak. SPENCER SWANGER

Above top, Pikes Peak is seen from the Garden of the Gods. ROBERT MACKINLAY

Gondola cars, right, slide horizontally across the yawning, 2,640-foot-wide abyss of the Royal Gorge. At the bottom lies Precambrian rock—the oldest in the region—dating back more than a billion years. JIM MARKHAM

Coyotes, above, howl at a wintery sky. MICHAEL S. SAMPLE

Wildflowers

Skunk cabbage, Indian paintbrush, larkspur, and a host of yellow composites, top, color the landscape of Pikes Peak. WILLIARD CLAY

Common in high alpine meadows, the bluish-purple flowers of the western fringed gentian, bottom, are invariably encountered by hikers. MICHAEL S. SAMPLE

Above, blue columbines complement Indian paintbrush for a rush of color. STEWART M. GREEN

One of the first flowers of spring, the yellow fritillary, top right, changes to red as the weeks progress. MICHAEL S. SAMPLE

Sand lily, above, blooms as early as April in sandy soil at lower elevations like the Garden of the Gods. MICHAEL S. SAMPLE

Green gentian, bottom left, is a favorite food of deer and elk.
MICHAEL S. SAMPLE

One of the earliest of bloomers in Pikes Peak Country, the pasque flower, bottom right, is often in full glory before Memorial Day.
MICHAEL S. SAMPLE

Pikes Peak trivia

▶ Lowell Thomas, famed news commentator, author, and lecturer, spent much of his early life in Victor. He began his newspaper career as a paperboy for the *Victor Record* and became the editor in 1911. He also worked in the mines as a mucker, ore sorter, assay carrier (taking samples from the mines to the mineral offices), and driller.

▶ Lon Chaney, star of dozens of horror films in the early part of the century, was born in Colorado Springs in 1886. His pantomime experience in communicating with his deaf parents prepared him for his start in show business as a vaudevillian. In 1923 he played the notorious Quasimodo in *The Hunchback of Notre Dame* and gained perhaps his greatest fame as the villain in *Phantom of the Opera* two years later.

▶ Jack Dempsey, heavyweight boxing champion of the world from 1919 to 1926, honed his pugilistic skills in Cripple Creek early in his career by boxing at night and mining during the day. Although his real name was William Harrison Dempsey, he first fought under the name of Jack Dempsey in Cripple Creek in 1915, knocking out George Copelin.

▶ Tom Mix, before making it big as a Hollywood Western actor, worked as a bartender on Bennett Avenue in Cripple Creek.

▶ Groucho Marx worked in the Pikes Peak region for a short time, delivering groceries between Victor and Cripple Creek. Groucho, who was 14 years old at the time, arrived in Cripple Creek in 1905 with a touring vaudeville act and became stranded when the two partners of his singing trio absconded with his savings. Forced to take a job, Groucho was fired in short order after his team of horses balked on a steep mountain pass between the two towns, necessitating the hiring of a more experienced driver. Groucho then wrote a letter to his mother explaining his dilemma, and she wired him the money to travel home to New York.

▶ The first wedding ever to take place at the summit of Pikes Peak was performed atop a steel tower on July 14, 1905.

▶ Bill Williams of Rio Hondo, Texas, pushed a peanut to the top of Pikes Peak with his nose during June 1929. In the course of the 22-mile, 20-day trip, he was reported to have worn out 170 pairs of pants, 12 pairs of gloves, and 3 pairs of shoes.

▶ Colorado Governor Teller Ammons bet Texas Governor Jimmy Allred the property of Pikes Peak against Big Bend National Park that the University of Colorado would beat Rice in the upcoming Cotton Bowl. Although Rice was victorious, 28-14 on the 1938 New Year's Day game, the Lone Star State governor never collected on his bet.

▶ The only bullfight ever staged in the United States took place in the town of Gillette in the Cripple Creek district on August 24, 1895. Held despite the objections of the U.S. government, the Humane Society, and church leaders, the event was billed as "the Great Mexican Bullfight." For the 3,000 people that gathered at a local racetrack to witness the event, it ended as quickly as it began when Mexican matador Jose Marrero killed the bull and promoter Joe Wolfe was arrested on charges of cruelty to animals.

▶ The mile-long Cave of the Winds in Williams Canyon is the only limestone cavern in Colorado that has been developed as a tourist attraction. It was formed by acidic groundwater that seeped through the fissures dissolving the limestone and forming enormous rooms. It is famous for its dazzling stalactites and stalagmites.

▶ A whale was reported on top of Pikes Peak in 1923. When reporters and photographers arrived to investigate, they found a 40-foot wooden whale that had been pieced together at the summit by a local promoter. Inside the whale was a man spraying seltzer through the blowhole.

▶ The second oil well in the United States—and the first west of the Mississippi River—was discovered on Oil Creek near Florence in 1862. The oil was said to have been hauled to Denver and sold as wagon grease.

► The Nature Place, a conference and outdoor center near Florissant, has been designated by the National Park Service as a National Environmental Study Area. The 6,000-acre property, staffed by geologists, biologists, historians, and artists, is part of the Colorado Outdoor Education Center.

► Irish Lord Sir George Gore, who passed through South Park during his three-year hunting excursion across the western United States from 1854-57, was a man of extremes. His entourage, made up of 40 men and guided by Jim Bridger, included 112 horses, 3 milk cows, 50 staghounds and greyhounds, and 2 entire wagonloads of fishing equipment. By Gore's own account, the party killed approximately 2,000 buffalo, 1,600 deer and elk, and 105 bears, spending over $500,000 and covering more than 6,000 miles in the process.

► When Zebulon Pike returned to the East following his stint in Pikes Peak Country, he earned a promotion to colonel shortly before the War of 1812. He died in an accident following the Battle of York in Ontario. The British had already surrendered, but an abandoned powder magazine exploded near Pike, throwing up a large rock that struck him in the back. He died a few hours later on a ship in Lake Ontario.

► For one dollar, thousands of sightseers took the one-day train trip from Colorado Springs to South Park and back via Elevenmile Canyon from the 1890s to 1918. Billed the Colorado Midland Wildflower Excursion, the tour was advertised by railroad employees' filling washtubs with columbines and placing them outside the ticket office in Manitou.

► Dr. A.G. Lewis homesteaded at the summit of Pikes Peak in the late 1880s. Although he apparently claimed his 160 acres in order to run a tourist shop for alpine travelers, he was nevertheless required by law to grow crops to validate his homestead. No problem. Lewis hauled dirt to the top and grew a few stunted vegetables. Upon the arrival of the cog railway in 1891, however, its developers acquired a 99-year lease on five acres on the summit for a terminal station, and the courts forced Lewis to give up his claim.

► In 1863 only one worshipper presented himself for the first church service ever held in Colorado City. The rest of the town had opted to attend the hanging of a horse thief. Following that act of frontier justice, the pious citizens trooped belatedly into church for a rousing sermon on "righteousness and judgement to come."

► "Don't jostle the man in the street," warned the *Cripple Creek Crusher*, the mining district's first newspaper, in 1895. "He may be a millionaire tomorrow and resent the insult."

► The price of gold per troy ounce was only $20.67 in 1900 when Winfield Scott Stratton was working his Independence Mine strike in the Cripple Creek district for $120,000 worth of ore a month.

► The Wright brothers, more renowned for their aerial exploits, once won an automobile race from Cripple Creek to Colorado Springs. They credited the victory to their stripping the car of unnecessary weight, then "hiking out" in sailing fashion in order to balance the vehicle around the sharp curves.

► The first Florence and Cripple Creek Railroad train, which arrived in the mining district on July 1, 1894, fell off of a trestle on its way back the following day, killing one person and injuring several others.

► Teddy Roosevelt was rescued from an angry mob in Victor in 1900. The vice-presidential nominee, who was campaigning for the Silver Republicans at the time, was met by a horde of William Jennings Bryant supporters shouting insults and carrying "Hang TR" banners. In the scuffle that followed, Roosevelt had his famous pincenez knocked from his nose. Only a two-by-four wielded by local Republican Danny Sullivan saved Roosevelt from further damage.

► The Cripple Creek mining district produced 30 millionaires in its heyday. One, a druggist, threw his hat in the air and started digging where it landed. From the spot rose the multimillion-dollar Pharmacist Mine.

► A number of motion pictures have been filmed in the Canon City area since 1948. They include *Canon City* (1948), *Vengeance Valley* (1951, starring Burt Lancaster), *The Outcast* (1953, starring John Derrick), *Big House, U.S.A.* (1954, starring Broderick Crawford), *Saddle the Wind* (1957, starring Robert Taylor and Julie London), *How the West was Won* (1962, starring James Arness), *Cat Ballou* (1964, starring Lee Marvin and Jane Fonda), *Then Came Bronson* (1969, starring Michael Parks), *The Cowboys* (1971, starring John Wayne), *Barquaro* (1972, starring Lee Van Cleef), *The Brothers O'Toole* (1972, starring John Astin), *True Grit* (1973, starring John Wayne), *Mr. Majestic* (1974, starring Charles Bronson), *The Duchess and Dirtwater Fox* (1975, starring Goldie Hawn), *Comes A Horseman* (1978, starring James Caan and Jane Fonda), and *The Sacketts* (1979, starring Tom Selleck and Sam Elliot).

► Canon City State Penitentiary's most famous prison break occurred in 1947 when 12 dangerous convicts broke out of the Isolation Section and slipped through the North Gate, scattering up Fourmile Canyon and Oak Creek. Within two weeks, with some of the men still at large, writing and technical crews from Hollywood were in town working on a motion picture based on the break. The movie, *Canon City*, was released in 1948.

► Bird Millman, probably the most famous high-wire artist of all time, was born in Canon City in 1890. During her career on the tightwire, she performed in London, Berlin, and Stockholm. Her greatest success, however, was with the Ringling Brothers-Barnum and Bailey Circus in the United States, where she was delivered to center stage in a white Rolls Royce before each performance.

► Parachutist Don Boyles of Tulsa, Oklahoma, made his 388th—and last—career parachute jump on September 7, 1970. It was a doozy. He leaped from the top of the Royal Gorge. After free-falling the first 150 feet of the 1,200-foot descent, Boyle floated down lazily the rest of the way, spraining his ankle during the rocky landing. Employees of the Royal Gorge Company were kind enough to give him a free ride to the top on the cog railway, but the company later threatened him with a $500 fine for "throwing objects from the bridge."

► South Cheyenne Canyon, which has been called the grandest mile of scenery in Colorado, is the only completely lighted canyon and waterfall in the world. Along the way can be seen the granite outcroppings known as the "Pillars of Hercules."

► Colorado Springs is a museum mecca. In addition to the Fine Arts Center, the area is also home to the Western Museum of Mining and Industry, the National Carvers Museum, the Numismatic Museum, the Clock Museum, the U.S. Figure Skating Museum, the Colorado Car Museum, Buffalo Bill's Wax Museum, the Hall of Presidents Wax Museum, the Cliff Dwellings Museum, the Ute Pass Museum, the American Cowboy Museum, the Edward J. Peterson Space Command Museum, the Wildlife World Museum, the McAllister House Historical Museum, the Pioneer Museum, the Miramont Castle Museum, the White House Ranch Museum, and the May Museum of Natural History.

► Of the 947 species of wildlife found in Colorado, approximately 80 percent are classified as nongame species that are not hunted or fished for and are protected by state statute. Of these, 23 are currently on the state's threatened and endangered list, including such Pikes Peak Country inhabitants as the greenback cutthroat trout, the bald eagle, and the peregrine falcon.

► Buckskin Joe, a mining community located near Fairplay, was moved to a site near the Royal Gorge in 1957. Originally reconstructed there as a movie set for Westerns, the town is now one of the top tourist attractions in the region, featuring such diversions as the reenactment of gunfights and authentic stagecoach rides.

► The Cheyenne Mountain Zoo overlooking Colorado Springs is a haven for endangered wildlife species. More orangutans have been born there than at any other zoo in the world, in addition to a host of lions, tigers, snow leopards, and jaguars. The zoo is currently the major supplier of giraffes to other zoos around the nation.

► The Broadmoor Hotel, erected in 1918 after the original Broadmoor Casino burned to the ground, is one of only eight resorts in America to be awarded

Mobil's distinguished five-star rating. The Broadmoor complex contains three hotels, three golf courses, a museum, and an ice arena.

▶ The May Museum, located just outside of Colorado Springs, is an entomologist's delight. With some 8,000 insects on display, rotated from a collection of more than 100,000 specimens, the fare includes 17-inch stick insects from New Guinea, 9-inch scorpions, a tarantula locked in a death grip with a hummingbird, and Columbian beetles so large that they have been known to knock people over when flying at speeds of 40 miles per hour.

▶ Members of the AdAmAn Club, who annually climb Pikes Peak on New Year's Eve to set off a fireworks display of flares, bombs, and mortars, made their first ascent for that purpose in 1921. The club, currently made up of 67 members, has been adding one member a year for the past 65 years.

▶ General William Jackson Palmer also founded Durango, Salida, Palmer Lake, South Pueblo, and Alamosa in addition to Colorado Springs. He was also responsible for founding Colorado College and the Colorado School for the Deaf and Blind. By developing new towns, Palmer was in fact finding ways to pay for his railroads.

▶ The Shelf Road, built soon after the gold discoveries at Cripple Creek, began business as a toll road with toll gates at the top and bottom. One-horse carriages were allowed to pass for 25 cents, while six-horse vehicles were charged one dollar. Livestock—apparently the best deal, pound for pound—was allowed to use the road for only a nickel a head.

▶ The highest navy in the world is said to be in the NORAD complex under Cheyenne Mountain. There, a single rowboat, complete with oars, serves the pair of reservoirs that have been built under the mountain.

▶ The late James Irwin, a Colorado Springs native and former astronaut, has gained nearly as much fame recently for his search for Noah's Ark as he did for his stroll on the moon in 1971. Irwin, who along with fellow astronaut David Scott were the first two astronauts to drive the Lunar Rover vehicle on the moon, has made six expeditions to Turkey's Mount Ararat in search of the Biblical ark in the 1980s.

Omnipresent at every turn, Pikes Peak casts a giant shadow over the entire region. STEPHEN TRIMBLE

A close-up of ponderosa pine bark reveals the intricacies of a surrealistic puzzle. MICHAEL S. SAMPLE

Strikingly similar to the much-photopraphed Half Dome in California's Yosemite Park, Dome Rock, top, is the landmark of Mueller State Park. W. PERRY CONWAY

Thirty miles northeast of Colorado Springs, 372 acres of grassland habitat surround 125-acre Ramah Reservoir, bottom, in El Paso County. CHARLES KNOECKEL

Pikes Peak framed by a red sandstone window. Just one of the many unusual and striking formations carved by nature in the Garden of the Gods. TOM TILL

The Broadmoor Hotel complex in Colorado Springs, top, illuminated by a flash of lightning. MICHAEL S. SAMPLE

The Rocky Mountain iris, bottom left, is unmistakable. The only species of iris that grows in the Rockies, it blooms from mid-May at the lower valleys to July in higher altitudes. MICHAEL S. SAMPLE

On Range View Road between Cripple Creek and Victor, an abandoned cabin, bottom right, marks life at the turn of the century. While the collective populations of Cripple Creek and Victor shrunk from 55,000 in 1900 to less than 1,000 in the late 1980s as a result of the district's played-out lodes, the legalization of limited-stakes gaming there by the Colorado State Legislature in 1991 has triggered an infusion of both people and cash into the historic towns. WENDY SHATTIL

Suggested Reading

Armstrong, David M. *Distribution of Mammals in Colorado*. Lawrence, Kans.: University of Kansas Printing Service, 1972.

Bailey, Alfred M. and Niedrach, Robert J. *Birds of Colorado*. Denver: Denver Museum of Natural History, 1965.

Carter, Harvey, ed. *The Pikes Peak Region: A Sesquicentennial History*. Colorado Springs: Historical Society of the Pikes Peak Region, 1956.

Cassells, E. Steve. *The Archaeology of Colorado*. Boulder: Johnson Books, 1983.

Chronic, Halka. *Roadside Geology to Colorado*. Missoula, Mont.: Mountain Press Publishing, 1980.

Chronic, John and Chronic, Halka. *Prairie, Peak, and Plateau*. Denver: Colorado Geologic Survey, 1972.

Colbert, Edwin H. *Men and Dinosaurs*. New York: Dutton, 1968.

Colorado Writers Program. *Colorado: A Guide to the Highest State*. Writer's Project of the Work Projects Administration. New York: Hastings House, 1941.

Craighead, John J., Craighead, Frank C., Jr., and Davies, Ray J. *A Field Guide To Rocky Mountain Wildflowers*. Boston: Houghton Mifflin Co., 1963.

Feitz, Leland. *Cripple Creek*. Colorado Springs: Little London Press, 1967.

——. *Victor, Colorado's City of Mines*. Colorado Springs: Little London Press, 1969.

Fetler, John. *The Pikes Peak People*. Caldwell, Idaho: The Caxton Printers, 1966.

Green, Stewart M. *Pikes Peak Country: The Complete Guide*. Colorado Springs: Ponderosa Press, 1985.

Hammerson, Geoffrey A. *Amphibians and Reptiles in Colorado*. Denver: Colorado Division of Wildlife, 1986.

Hart, Stephan and Hulbert, Archer. *Zebulon Pike's Arkansaw Journal*. Westport, Conn.: Greenwood Press, 1972.

Hendren, Frederick M. *Pikes Peak Legacy*. Colorado Springs: Great Western Press, 1984.

Lechleitner, R.R. *Wild Mammals of Colorado*. Boulder: Pruett Publishing Co., 1969.

Levine, Brian H. *Cities of Gold: History and Tales of the Cripple Creek Mining District*. Colorado Springs: Century One Press, 1981.

Mutel, Cornelia Fleischer and Emerick, John C. *From Grassland to Glacier*. Boulder: Johnson Books, 1984.

Pearl, Richard M. *America's Gem Trails*. New York: McGraw-Hill Book Co., 1964.

——. *America's Mountain*. Denver: Sage Books, 1964.

——. *Exploring Rocks, Minerals, and Fossils in Colorado*. Chicago: Sage Books, 1969.

Rennicke, Jeff. *Colorado Mountain Ranges*. Helena, Mont.: Falcon Press, 1986.

——. *The Rivers of Colorado*. Helena, Mont.: Falcon Press, 1985.

Simmons, Virginia McConnell. *Bayou Salado: The Story of South Park*. Denver: Sage Books, 1966.

Sprague, Marshall. *Money Mountain: The History of Cripple Creek Gold*. Boston: Little, Brown, 1953.

——. *Newport in the Rockies*. Chicago: Sage Books, 1961.

Falcon Press-*Your Guide to Colorado Adventures*

Falcon Press brings you the best of Colorado—whether you want a momento of your vacation or a reminder of your home state. Falcon Press books send you on scenic drives, take you on adventurous hikes, and lead you to the best bike trails.

Or, if you're an armchair traveler, you have Colorado at your fingertips! Outstanding photos of wildlife, parks and mountains, and lively text transport you to the heart of the Rockies.

Falcon Press books also make the perfect gift. *Colorado on My Mind*, part of Falcon Press's award-winning On My Mind series showcases photographic excellence. Each image brings Colorado to life. Each photo tells a story. Piece together the fascinating story of Colorado with this and all our other books that help keep Colorado on your mind and in your heart.

Colorado Books From Falcon Press

C is for Colorado
Colorado Mountain Ranges
Colorado on My Mind
Colorado Parklands
The Hiker's Guide to Colorado
The Mountain Biker's Guide to Colorado
Colorado Postcard Book
Colorado Scenic Drives

Colorado Ski Country
Colorado Wildflowers
Colorado Wildlife
Colorado Wildlife Viewing Guide
The Floater's Guide to Colorado
It Happened in Colorado
The Rivers of Colorado
San Juan Skyway

For more information about these and other Falcon Press books contact your local bookstore.
Or call toll-free
1-800-582-2665

FALCO